CAUSES AND CONSEQUENCES
OF THE
ARAB-ISRAELI
CONFLICT

CAUSES AND CONSEQUENCES
OF THE
ARAB-ISRAELI CONFLICT

STEWART ROSS

Evans

CAUSES AND CONSEQUENCES
The First World War
The Second World War
The Arab-Israeli Conflict

Revised edition published in paperback in 2004 by
Evans Brothers Limited
2A Portman Mansions
Chiltern Street
London W1U 6NR
England

© Evans Brothers Limited 1995.

British Library Cataloguing in Publication Data
Ross, Stewart
Causes and consequences of the Arab-Israeli conflict
1. Israel-Arab conflicts - Juvenile literature
2. Jewish-Arab relations - 1949 - Juvenile literature
I. Title II Arab-Israeli conflict
956'. 042

ISBN 0237525852

First published in 1995 reprinted 1998

Planning and production by the Creative Publishing Company
Edited by Sabrina Crewe
Designed by Ian Winton

This book is gratefully dedicated to Lings Upper School, Northampton, in particular to those who helped with the captions: Charlotte Armstrong, Laura Brown, Sophie Coleman, Sophie Holtham, Rebecca Porter, Sarah Smith and Matthew Smithers.

ACKNOWLEDGEMENTS

The publishers are grateful to the following for permission to reproduce photographs:

Corbis: front cover, pages 6, 7, 48, 49, 50, 55, 60, 61, 62, 64, 65, 66, 67, 71, 72
Hulton Getty: pages 20, 22, 32, 36, 37, 38, 40, 44, 45, 53
Imperial War Museum: 35
Magnum Photos: pages 31, 33, 42, 47, 51, 58
Popperfoto: pages 8, 12, 13, 17
Range/Bettmann: pages 16, 41
Range/Bettmann/UPI: pages 23, 25, 28, 29, 52, 56, 70
Range/Reuter/Bettmann: page 57
Rex Features: page 68
United Nations: page 63
UPI/Bettmann: page 59

CONTENTS

THE WORLD'S ANGRY REGION

A land divided: the Israeli-built 'security fence' that divides much of the Palestinian West Bank from the state of Israel. The line of the fence, as well as the very idea of it, has caused bitter dispute.

Since the end of the Second World War in 1945, scarcely a day has passed when the Middle East has not been in the news. For decades the reporting has been largely of tragedy – war, terrorism, hostages and destruction. Occasionally, especially since 1978, announcements have struck a more positive note, talking of troop withdrawals and peace settlements. Every now and again, commentators speak of 'breakthrough' and 'lasting peace', but such optimism has proved to be misplaced.

Two peoples lie at the heart of the Middle East problem, Israelis and Palestinians. The latter are part of a much larger racial group, the Arabs. The Arabs are not a nation. They are a people, united by a common language, history and culture. They do not all share

the same faith. Although most are Muslims, many millions, notably in Lebanon, are Christian. Arabs make up the bulk of the population in Morocco, Algeria and Libya in north Africa, and the majority of the countries of the Middle East.

Until the middle of the twentieth century most Arabs outside the remote desert regions of Arabia lived under the imperial rule of Turkey, France or Britain. As this rule crumbled, independent Arab states emerged. At the height of this process however, just after the Second World War, the Arab world was infuriated by an unprecedented event. Without Arab consent

A giant statue of Saddam Hussein is toppled after the US-led coalition removed him from power as part of its 'war on terror', 2003. Many Americans believed the war should move on to tackle Palestinian attacks on Israeli targets.

7

We accept no kind of co-existence with Israel. The rights of the Palestinians should be given back to them. What happened in 1948 was an aggression against the people of Palestine. Israel expelled the Palestinians from their country and stole their property.

President Gamel Adbul Nasser of Egypt, 28 May 1967

a new, non-Arab state was founded within Palestine, a territory previously governed by the British. The new state was Israel. The day of its foundation, 14 May 1948, was the day the Arab-Israeli conflict began.

Israel was established as a homeland for the Jewish people. Like the Arabs, the Jews are a people rather than a nation. They too are bound together by language, culture, history and, more than the Arabs, by religion. In ancient times they inhabited the Biblical land of Israel, at the eastern end of the Mediterranean. But during the rule of the Romans, which culminated in a failed uprising against their imperial masters in 67 AD, most Jewish people left their historic homeland of Israel and settled all over Europe and the Middle East. This process is known as the dispersal or *Diaspora*.

For centuries the Jews lived in widespread communities in different parts of the world. A few never left their ancestral territory, which became the district of Palestine within the Ottoman (Turkish) province of Syria. Elsewhere, Jewish communities grew up in most Arab and European lands. More recently, they settled in the Americas and the Far East. Historically, they were blamed for having put Jesus Christ to death and from time to time they were subjected to harsh persecution, particularly in Christian countries and in the lands occupied by the Nazis. Because of their distinctive dress and customs and because they did not always readily mix with people of other races, they were an easily-distinguished minority. Criticized when they achieved commercial success, they were frequently made scapegoats for ills

The persecuted people of Europe — Jews being led away to Nazi extermination camps following the collapse of the rising in the Warsaw ghetto, 1943.

which were beyond their control, such as famine and economic recession.

Since the Diaspora, certain Jewish leaders had never abandoned the rather romantic notion that one day they would return to a homeland in the Middle East. From the late nineteenth century onwards this idea – known as Zionism – received increasing support. It was not an ambition unique to the Jews. In many parts of the world people of the same culture and background, including Arabs, were aspiring to their own nation state. But the situation in the Middle East was complicated when Britain, eager for support against Turkey in World War I, appeared to promise a Palestinian homeland to both Jews and Palestinians. Finally, with the backing of the victors of World War II, it was the Jews who got what they wanted – Israel.

The consequences of this action rumble on to this day. It destabilized the Middle East, making it perhaps the most troubled region in the world; it united – and divided – the Arabs; it left a large number of Palestinian Arabs as second class citizens in an alien state; it drove the Palestinians to form their own resistance organizations (see Chapter Nine) dedicated to opposing the Israelis by any means possible, including terrorism; it made many of the citizens of the new state suspicious, intolerant and defensive; it bred major wars, two long bloody uprisings, and hundreds of horrifying terrorist attacks; it wracked and distorted the economies of Israel and her neighbours; it brought the United States close to confrontation with the Soviet Union; it led to an oil embargo that rocked the world economy; it brought assassination, torture and the downfall of politicians.

At the same time, it led to a quest for peace. The process began to bear fruit in the 1970s, initiated by the United States and President Sadat of Egypt. Gradually, led by Jordan, other Arab states joined the process. Tragically, this peace process failed to meet the demands of those who had suffered most since the troubles began – the Palestinian Arabs. By resorting to violence, this homeless and desperate people drew attention to their plight and caused others to attempt to mediate a peaceful solution to their problem. Whether these efforts will succeed, and thereby finally end the Arab-Israeli conflict, only time will tell. But for the moment no picture of the modern world is complete without an understanding of the causes and consequences of this most bitter of conflicts.

President Carter once said that the United States is committed without reservation to seeing the peace process through until all parties to the Arab-Israeli conflict are at peace. We value such a promise from a leader who raised the banners of morality as a substitute for power politics and opportunism.

President Anwar Sadat of Egypt, 26 March 1979

TWO PEOPLES, ONE LAND

THE NATION STATE

The Turkish Ottoman Empire at the outbreak of the First World War in 1914. The break up of the empire after the war created the opportunity for a Jewish homeland in Palestine.

Over the last hundred years politicians of every continent have divided just about the entire land surface of the world into countries, or nation states. There are almost two hundred separate nation states, each with its own flag, government and national identity. Its people generally share a similar racial, cultural and religious background. Where they do not do so, the state runs the risk of splitting into a number of smaller states. This happened to the Soviet Union, Yugoslavia and Czechoslovakia in the 1990s.

The nation state is a relatively new concept. In the Middle Ages, for example, the people of Europe had a sense of belonging to Christendom as much as to a

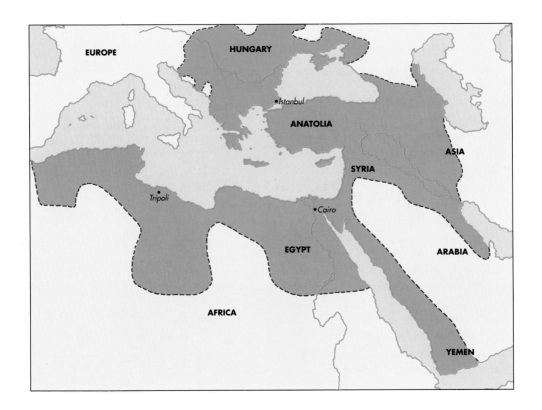

particular kingdom. Similarly, the Arab people thought of themselves as members of the Muslim world. For Africans the tribe was the focus of loyalty, not a country.

Although there have been countries with a strong sense of national unity since medieval times, the true age of the nation state began in the nineteenth century. By 1880 the small states and cities of Germany and Italy had joined together to form single nations. Further east, the subject peoples of the Ottoman Empire began to break away from Turkish rule and form nations of their own. Western imperialist powers gathered colonies around the world. When these colonies acquired independence in the twentieth century, they too became new nation states. The two great international organizations of the twentieth century, the League of Nations and the United Nations, were based on membership of nation states. Pride in one's nation, or nationalism, became a major political force.

The search for nationhood affected all peoples. Those without a nation of their own were seen as 'stateless', second class citizens. Consequently, they felt a powerful need to belong, to create a nation state of their own. No two peoples have felt this need more strongly than the Jews and the Palestinians.

The reawakening of the Arab nation, and the mounting efforts of the Jews to rebuild the ancient monarchy of Israel on a massive scale — these two movements are bound to fight continually, until one defeats the other.

N Azouri, *The Awakening of the Arab Nation Against the Asian Turk*, 1905

PALESTINE

Palestine is the area of land between the River Jordan and the Mediterranean. To the north it is bounded by Lebanon, to the south by the Neger and Sinai deserts. In Biblical times the area lay at the heart of the Jewish kingdom of King Solomon, commonly known as Israel. Palestine is sometimes termed the Holy Land because certain places, notably the city of Jerusalem, played a special part in the Jewish, Muslim and Christian religions. After the First World War this area of land was freed from centuries of Turkish rule, made a mandate by the League of Nations and named Palestine.

Some historians claim, controversially, that the Jews and Palestinian Arabs are descended from the same racial stock. Whether this is true or not there have always been Jews and Arabs living in the Palestine region. In 637AD the area was conquered by the Muslim Arabs, who treated their Jewish neighbours relatively well. The Christian Crusaders, who held various parts of Palestine from 1099 until 1291, persecuted the Jews mercilessly by comparison. The region was then governed by Turkish Muslims, first the Mamluks (1291-1516), then the Ottomans (1517-1917). The Turks tolerated the Jewish religion, and even welcomed Jewish refugees from Christian persecution in Europe. Some estimates suggest that by 1800 the majority of the population of Jerusalem were Jews. Although there were sporadic incidents of racial and religious unrest, Jews and Arabs lived for centuries in relative harmony under their Turkish masters.

JEWISH AND ARAB NATIONALISM

In the later nineteenth century two movements arose which shattered the harmony of Palestine and laid the foundations for the Arab-Israeli conflict. These movements were Jewish nationalism (also known as Zionism after *Zion*, the ancient Jewish name for Jerusalem) and Arab nationalism. In other words, both the Arabs and the Jews wanted self-rule in their own nation state.

Theodore Herzl (1860–1904), the Austrian Jew who called the first Zionist Congress at Basel in 1897, launching the movement for an independent Jewish homeland.

The modern movement for a Jewish homeland was provoked by a series of violent attacks, known as pogroms, on the Jews in Russia in the early 1880s. In

1882 a group of Jewish exiles met in Constantinople. Calling themselves 'Lovers of Zion', they issued a powerful manifesto in which they called for 'a home in our country. It was given to us by the mercy of God; it is ours as registered in the archives of history.'

These people believed that God had given Palestine to the Jews. The problem was that by 1880 most inhabitants of Palestine were Arabs, not Jews. Herein lay the seeds of future conflict.

Zionism became a political movement under the leadership of an Austrian Jew named Theodore Herzl (1860-1904), who organized Zionist conferences and set out his plans in a pamphlet entitled *The Jewish State*. A World Zionist

Jewish immigrants to Palestine building the new town of Tel Aviv, founded 1909. Arabs watched the construction of the first entirely Jewish town with dismay.

Organization was formed in 1897 and the number of Jews emigrating to Palestine increased quite sharply. Some sources (probably favouring Jewish claims to Israel) say that between 1880 and 1914 over 60,000 Jews arrived, mostly from Eastern Europe. The population of Palestine by 1914 has been estimated at half a million Arabs and between 50,000 and 90,000 Jews.

In 1909 an entirely Jewish town, Tel Aviv, was founded alongside the port of Jaffa. This marked a worrying trend – the separation of Jew from Arab. The immigrants bought land, often from Arabs, and established their own communities. Only in the large cities – Gaza, Hebron, Safed, Tiberias and Jerusalem – did the two peoples live side by side.

Palestinian nationalism did not emerge as a major force until after the Second World War. But a more general movement, Arab nationalism, began to make itself felt in the first years of the twentieth century. It found a voice in the journalist Negib Azouri, editor of a magazine called *Arab Independence* which supported a League of the Arab Fatherland. Azouri wanted the Arab peoples released from Turkish rule and free to govern themselves in an Arab empire. Although he preached religious toleration, the concept of an Arab Fatherland did not accord well with what was happening in Palestine.

In 1886 the first attack by Arabs on Jewish settlements occurred. Five years later a group of Palestinian Arabs petitioned the Turkish government in Constantinople to halt Jewish immigration into Palestine. In 1914 six anti-Zionist societies were set up, four in Palestine and one each in Beirut and Constantinople.

The Jewish question is . . . a national question. We are a people — one people. Wherever we have lived, we have honestly tried to mix in socially with other people, while at the same time keeping our religion. But we have not been allowed to do this . . . .

The answer, therefore, is simple . . . . Give us control over part of the globe big enough to meet the Jews' rightful needs; the rest we shall manage for ourselves.

Theodore Herzl, *The Jewish State*, 1896

BROKEN PROMISES

BRITAIN AND THE MIDDLE EAST

Just when tension between the Arabs and Jews in Palestine was beginning to look sinister, the situation was suddenly complicated further by the outbreak of the First World War. The Arab world became involved on 5 November 1914, when Britain declared war on Turkey, an ally of Germany. Neither France nor Russia (Britain's allies) were in a position to commit troops to the Middle East. Britain already had a strong interest in the region, controlling Egypt and key points at the southern end of the Arabian peninsular. This control was essential to safeguard the Suez Canal and the route to India, Britain's most valued colony. The British were also eager to see that the

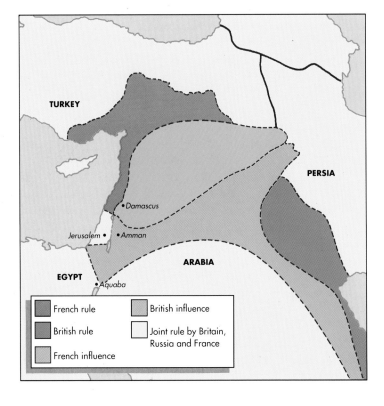

The Sykes-Picot Agreement of 1916 was a secret plan to divide the captured Ottoman lands into five territories, but it made no provision for a Jewish homeland. Although a crucial part of Anglo-French negitiations, the Sykes-Picot plan was never used.

TURKEY

PERSIA

• Damascus

Jerusalem • • Amman

ARABIA

EGYPT

• Aquaba

■ French rule		■ British influence	
■ British rule		□ Joint rule by Britain, Russia and France	
■ French influence			

Middle East oil fields did not fall into hostile hands, and so they undertook to oppose the Turks.

Britain's task was daunting. Ottoman territory in the Middle East stretched from Turkey itself to Akaba and Mecca in the west and Basra at the head of the Persian Gulf in the east. Moreover, the Turks had held their Arab empire for centuries. They knew it intimately and were experienced at fighting in its arid regions. The sort of setback feared by the British happened in April 1916, when the Turks forced the surrender of an Anglo-Indian force at Kut, in Mesopotamia (now Iraq). The British had already realized that to have any hope of success, they needed an ally. And realistically there was only one choice – the Arabs.

BRITAIN AND THE ARABS

Britain's approach to the Arabs was made through its High Commissioner in Cairo, Sir Henry McMahon. The man he chose to negotiate with was Hussein Ibn Ali, the Sherif of Mecca, who hoped to be the first leader of an independent Arab State. From the British he sought recognition of his claim and a joint operation against the Turks.

A number of letters passed between the two men, the most important of which was written by McMahon on 24 October 1915. It was carefully constructed and began by excluding from any agreement the 'portions of Syria lying to the west of the district[s] of Damascus . . . [as they] cannot be said to be purely Arab.' It also said that Britain could not be bound by any agreement that might run against French interests. 'Subject to the above modifications,' it went on, 'Great Britain is prepared to recognize and support the independence of the Arabs in all the regions within the limits demanded by the Sherif of Mecca.'

This sentence was the key. Armed with it, Hussein raised a powerful Arab force and by September 1918 he and the British under General Allenby had defeated the Turks and entered Damascus. The time had come, Hussein demanded, for the British to honour their promises to him. But it was not to be.

The British pointed out the reservations in McMahon's letter. They also referred to other letters between the High Commissioner and Hussein, which had failed to resolve who should control the area to the west of the River Jordan. The words 'Palestine',

Major General Edmund Allenby (1861-1936), the British commander who was moved from the Western front to the Middle East in 1917. His skilful campaign against the Turks led to the capture of Jerusalem and Damascus.

'Jerusalem' and 'Jews' had never been specifically mentioned by either party.

But if that was bad for Hussein, there was worse to come. During the war Britain had made two other agreements regarding the Middle East that seemed to contradict the pledge made to the Sherif of Mecca.

BRITAIN AND FRANCE

Shortly after the outbreak of the First World War, Britain and France started negotiating on the fate of the post-war Ottoman Empire. They assumed, of course, that they would win. A secret plan, known as the Sykes-Picot Agreement, was prepared by Sir Mark Sykes and Charles Georges-Picot in 1916.

The Sykes-Picot Agreement divided the Ottoman Arab lands into five categories. Some were to be under direct French or British rule, other parts were designated Arab states, but under British or French 'influence'. Finally, a region (roughly the area of Palestine) around the Holy Places was to be under the joint control of Britain, Russia and France. There was no mention of a separate homeland for the Jews, but nor was there any attempt to honour the understanding entered into with Hussein. A third promise, delivered the year after the Sykes-Picot agreement, made the situation even more complicated.

BRITAIN AND THE JEWS

1917 was a hard year for Britain. The war seemed to be dragging on for ever, at a huge cost in men, materials and money. In November, Arthur Balfour (1848-1930), the British Foreign Minister, sent a letter to Lord Rothschild, a prominent Jewish banker and supporter of Zionism. In the letter Balfour offered his government's support for 'the establishment in Palestine of a national home for the Jewish people'.

Ever since, people have wondered why the Balfour Declaration was made. It contradicted the Sykes-Picot agreement and the understanding

Arthur James Balfour (centre), the British Foreign Secretary whose famous Balfour Declaration of 1917 promised a national home for the Jews in Palestine and appeared to run contrary to previous British undertakings to their Arab allies. The figure second from the right is Dr Chaim Weizmann (1874–1952), the Zionist leader credited with a prominent role in securing the Declaration.

between Hussein and McMahon. Three reasons for Balfour's behaviour have been suggested. Firstly, Britain was wooing prominent Jews, whose support was needed at home, in the United States and in Russia. Secondly, it is thought that Balfour wanted a state friendly to Britain in the eastern Mediterranean, to safeguard the Suez Canal and act as a buffer between French-controlled Syria and British-controlled Egypt. Finally, the Zionist leader Chaim Weizmann got on well with the leading members of the British government, many of whom felt sorry for the Jews and wished to help them.

THE MANDATES

By the time the First World War ended, therefore, Britain had made three different and, some may say, contradictory proposals: (1) to help the Arabs set up their own states in the Middle East; (2) to divide the region between Britain and France; and (3) to give the Jews their own 'national home' in Palestine. At the 1919 peace talks, it was an Anglo-French plan — though not the Sykes-Picot agreement — which was finally accepted. The former Ottoman Arab lands were put in the hands of Britain and France, who were to look after them and prepare them for self-government. Britain received Iraq, Transjordan and Palestine, while France was given Syria and Lebanon. Iraq became independent in 1932, Lebanon and Syria in 1944 and Transjordan in 1946. In taking over Palestine, however, the British had landed themselves with a problem for which they had no solution.

An answer seemed to be to divide Palestine into two states, one Arab and the other Jewish. In 1919 this appeared to have been agreed between Chaim Weizmann and Hussein's son, Faisal, who later became King of Iraq. However other Arab leaders rejected the plan, and in 1929 Faisal himself said that he had come to no such understanding. Sporadic fighting between Jews and Arabs broke out in 1920. The following year the British correctly stated that they had never intended the whole of Palestine to become a Jewish 'home'. But the time for compromise had passed. After the three different proposals of the war years, neither the Jews nor the Arabs trusted their British overlords. A full-blown Arab-Jewish conflict in Palestine was now a distinct possibility.

We Arabs, especially the educated among us, look with the deepest sympathy on the Zionist movement. [We are] . . . fully acquainted with the proposals submitted yesterday [2 March 1919] by the Zionist Organization to the Peace Conference, and we regard them as moderate and proper. We will do out best . . . to help them through: we will wish the Jews a most hearty welcome home.

Letter from Faisal ibn Hussein to the leader of the Jewish delegation at the 1919 Versailles Peace Conference, 3 March 1919. (Faisal later denied authorship)

THE WEAK POLICEMAN

THE BRITISH IN PALESTINE

In theory the League of Nations was responsible for the former German and Turkish colonies taken over as mandates after the First World War. In practice it handed over this responsibility to certain of the victorious nations, in effect adding to those nations' already large colonial empires.

In many ways Britain was not the right country to be given responsibility for overseeing Palestine and bringing it to self-government. Britain's primary interest in the region was not fulfilling the wishes of the local people, but safeguarding the Suez Canal and the route to India. Furthermore, by her deeds and actions during the war, Britain had lost the trust of both the Arab and Jewish communities.

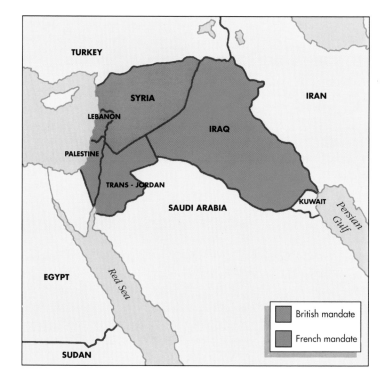

The Middle East mandates after the First World War, which gave responsibility for Palestine and some of its neighbours to Britain and France. Egypt remained a British Protectorate until 1922.

To deal with the ex-Turkish provinces not considered ready for independence, British Colonial Secretary Winston Churchill (front row, centre) called the Cairo Conference of 1921. Also in attendance are TE Lawrence ('Lawrence of Arabia', fourth from the right, second row) and Sir Herbert Samuel, on Churchill's right.

Arab hopes had been raised by McMahon's declaration of support for Arab independence, then dashed by his government's failure to follow this up. The Arabs had been further annoyed by the Balfour Declaration and the apparent support for the Jewish cause among leading British politicians. An example of this support came in 1921 when the British Colonial Secretary Winston Churchill declared '. . . it is manifestly right that the Jews, who are scattered all over the world, should have a . . . National Home where some of them may be united. Where else could this be but in this land of Palestine, with which for more than three thousand years they have been intimately and profoundly associated? We think it will be good for the world, good for the Jews and good for the British Empire.'

The Jews, too, had reason to mistrust the British. The Balfour Declaration, which directly contradicted the Sykes-Picot agreement, seemed to them a cynical bid for support at a time when British fortunes were at a low ebb. In the period of the British mandate over Palestine (1920–48) the fears of both Arab and Jew were fuelled by Britain's indecisive and wavering attitude. Sometimes, such as when they set limits on Jewish immigration, they appeared to support the Arabs. More often, particularly in their treatment of Arab resistance, it looked as if they were backing the Jews.

Above all, the British seemed to have no policy towards Palestine other than trying to contain the violence. In the light of the Arab-Israeli agreements reached in the 1990s, probably the only solution would have been to have divided Palestine between Arab and Jewish areas as soon as the mandate had been established. Although suggested, this was never done. As a result, Britain was seen as a weak and biased policeman unable to control a beat for which he was not really concerned, and British officials and soldiers became targets for both sides. Britain's inept handling of the problems of the mandate, therefore, was a major cause of the future Arab-Israeli conflict.

IMMIGRATION AND RESISTANCE

One of Britain's first mistakes was to appoint a Jew, Sir Herbert Samuel, as High Commissioner of Palestine. He held the post until 1925. His report on leaving his post made quite clear where his sympathies lay. When he arrived in Palestine, he recalled, the Valley of Jezreel 'was a desolation'. All he saw were 'four or five squalid Arab villages'. Otherwise there was 'not a house, not a tree'. In contrast, by 1925, after five years of Jewish settlement and an investment of almost a million Egyptian pounds, 'the whole aspect of the valley has been changed . . . . In the spring the fields of vegetables or of cereals cover many miles of land, and what five years ago was little better than a desert is being transformed before our eyes into smiling countryside.' The words 'squalid' and 'smiling', contrasting Arab and Jewish lifestyles, do not suggest an unbiased viewpoint.

Britain's problems began in 1920, when Arabs attacked Jewish settlements and caused four of them to be abandoned. By the end of the year it is believed about 10,000 Jewish immigrants had arrived in Israel since the end of the First World War. They established their own defence force, the Haganah, and the General Federation of Jewish Labour, which promoted further immigration and settlement. The Arabs asked the British to establish Palestinian self-rule before the Jews gained an even stronger hold over the land. The British refused, but in September 1920 they limited Jewish immigration to 16,500 a year; the following

So far as the Arabs are concerned . . . I hope they will remember that it is we who have established an independent Arab sovereignty of the Hedjaz [Arabia]. I hope they will remember it is we who desire in Mesopotamia [Iraq] to prepare the way for . . . a self-governing . . . Arab state, and I hope that, remembering all that, they will not grudge that small notch — for it is no more than that geographically, whatever it may be historically — that small notch in what are now Arab territories being given to the people [the Jews] who for all these hundreds of years have been separated from it.'

Arthur Balfour, 12 July 1920

A city at peace — Jerusalem, 1925. During the mid-1920s Arab and Jew co-existed in relative harmony.

The Jew is clannish and unneighbourly, and cannot mix with those who live about him. He will enjoy the privileges and benefits of a country and then lead its people, whom he has already impoverished, where he chooses. He encourages wars when self-interest dictates, and thus uses the armies of the nations to do his bidding.

Letter from the Haifa Congress of Palestinian Arabs to Winston Churchill, 28 March 1921

year all immigration was temporarily suspended. However it is estimated that the Jewish population of Palestine doubled between 1918 and 1929. In 1929 an official British estimate suggested that if Jews entered Palestine at the rate of 15,000 a year, the Jewish population would equal that of the Arabs by 1956. It is often forgotten that the Jews were not the only immigrants into Palestine — figures indicate 50,000 Arabs also entered the country between 1919 and 1939.

Racial tension died down at the end of 1921 but flared up again in 1929 with a series of anti-Jewish riots, some marked by extreme cruelty. Once again the British were caught in the middle. The Jerusalem riots of 23 August 1929 left 133 Jews and 116 Arabs dead. Of the latter, 110 had been killed by the British police. While the Arabs accused the British of treating them like 'naughty children', the Jews said the mandate government deprived them of the means to defend themselves, 'giving the murderers and robbers their chance'.

In 1936 the Arabs began a general strike in which they were led by their spiritual leader, the Grand Mufti of Jerusalem. This was followed by a major anti-Jewish and anti-British uprising. The country descended into chaos as Arabs attacked Jews, the

British and even fellow Arabs who sympathized with the Jewish cause, and Jews fought back against the Arabs. The British moved 20,000 troops into the region to restore order. One British officer, Orde Wingate, even organized Jewish Special Night Squads to attack Arab villages. It was hardly the sort of move that would bring peace or allay Arab fears. The squads' tactics were often as brutal and destructive as anything practised by the Arabs.

By the later 1930s, therefore, the British had failed to control Arab-Jewish hostility, which was approaching new heights of ferocity. Furthermore, in central Europe a series of events was already underway that would change Palestine's internal problem into a war between nations. In 1933 the Nazis came to power in Germany and the last seed of the future Arab-Israeli conflict was sown.

Wingate . . . went up to the four Arab prisoners. He said in Arabic, 'You have arms in the village. Where have you hidden them?' The Arabs shook their heads. Wingate reached down and took sand from the ground. He thrust it into the mouth of the first Arab and pushed it down until he puked.

Cited in Walter Oppenheim, *The Middle East*, Blackwell, 1989

A city in turmoil — Jaffa, 1933. Arabs demonstrating against Jewish immigration into Palestine confront British police. Some forty people, British and Arab, were killed.

PERSECUTION AND PARTITION

THE HOLOCAUST

The Jews had been persecuted throughout the history of Christian Europe. Individuals, families, even whole communities had been beaten up or killed and their property stolen or destroyed. Sometimes a country had expelled all Jews living there. But nothing in Europe's past equalled the sickening horror of Nazi anti-Semitism. Beginning with discrimination in 1933, it grew to vicious persecution and ended with the Holocaust — a cold-blooded attempt to exterminate the entire Jewish race from Nazi-held lands. Estimates of the number of Jews killed vary from five to eleven million.

Nazi anti-Semitism raised two emotions in the hearts of the leaders of the Western powers — guilt and sympathy. Both ensured that after the war they swung strongly behind the Palestinian Jews and supported the foundation of the state of Israel. When the awful truth of what had been going on in the slaughter pits and extermination camps of the Third Reich became apparent, Western sympathy for the Jews was immediate and understandable. The West's guilt, however, requires some explanation.

Between 1933 and 1945 the countries in a position to shelter refugees from Nazi persecution put concerns about domestic unemployment above humanitarian assistance. Brazil, Spain, Australia and South Africa, for example, placed severe limits on Jewish immigration. India, Turkey and Mexico were virtually closed. Britain and the United States limited by quota systems the numbers of refugees they would accept. In 1941 the United States Congress rejected a proposal to stretch the quota to allow the entry of 20,000 German-Jewish children. Two years later the British government rejected an appeal by the Archbishop of Canterbury to abolish its quota system. In the same year the United States State Department turned down a Swedish plan to rescue another 20,000 Jewish children from Germany.

(I) That Jew shall not dominate Arab and Arab shall not dominate Jew in Palestine. (II) That Palestine shall be neither a Jewish nor an Arab state. (III) That the form of government ultimately to be established, shall under international guarantees, fully protect and preserve the interests in the Holy Land of Christendom and of the Moslem and Jewish faiths.

Recommendations of the Anglo-American Committee of Enquiry into the condition of the Jewish people, 1 May 1945

The most poignant example of the manner in which Jewish refugees were shunned by officialdom was the story of the voyage of the liner *St Louis*. Carrying 930 Jewish refugees, on 13 May 1939 the ship left Germany bound for the United States of America. Most of the passengers had permission to enter the United States within three years, and all held Cuban landing certificates. However, the Cubans permitted only twenty-two to come ashore. The USA accepted not one. Its example was followed by several South American countries. In June the ship returned to Europe, where Britain, Holland and Belgium agreed to take the refugees. Those who ended up in mainland Europe came under Nazi rule within the year. Many were exterminated. The 287 who had landed in Britain were imprisoned as 'enemy aliens' on the outbreak of war. In the light of tales such as this, it is hardly surprising that the appeal for a Jewish homeland was favourably received in 1945. The Arab cause was not helped by the fact that their leader, the Mufti of Jerusalem, had been friendly with Hitler.

Jewish families prepare to flee the Baltic port of Memel in March 1939, as German troops move in and the Nazi swastika is raised over Jewish homes.

THE LAST DAYS OF PALESTINE

Nazi persecution increased the number of Jewish refugees seeking entry into Palestine. This in turn fuelled Arab-Jewish tension and made Britain's task of

DER EWIGE JUDE

GROSSE POLITISCHE SCHAU IM BIBLIOTHEKSBAU DES DEUTSCHEN MUSEUMS

An anti-Semitic poster from a Nazi exhibition of 1937, entitled 'The Eternal Jew'. The persecution of Jews aroused sympathy and guilt around the world, leading many countries to support the foundation of Israel.

governing the Palestinian mandate even more difficult.

The fighting of 1936 continued into 1938 and 1939. As well as employing peace-keeping forces, Britain also tried to stop the fighting by diplomatic means. A Royal Commission was set up in 1936 to report on how the government of the mandate was progressing. The result was the Peel Commission Report of 1937. It recommended that Palestine be divided into three parts: a small Jewish state in the north, a large Arab state in the south, and a small tongue of land stretching from the coast to the Holy Places remaining under British control. The Jews reluctantly accepted the proposal. The Arabs rejected it outright. They would not surrender a single piece of land that was, they claimed, inherently theirs. The terrorism carried out by both sides went on.

Another way the British tried to settle the disturbances was to limit Jewish immigration and land purchase. In 1935 it is thought that over 60,000 Jews entered Palestine. (Precise figures are very hard to come by because Jewish figures underestimated the number of immigrants, Arab figures were overestimates and British figures discounted the number of illegal immigrants.) This figure was halved in 1936 and further reduced in 1937 and 1938. It rose again to perhaps 30,000 in 1939, by which time dozens of new Jewish settlements had been established.

In 1939 British policy changed. Jewish immigration was cut back to about 4,000 a year and subsequent illegal immigrants were deported to Cyprus and Mauritius. In February 1940, huge areas of Palestine were delineated in which no further Jewish settlement was permitted. An independent Palestine, shared between Arabs and Jews, was planned for 1949. The British had, in essence, washed their hands of the problem, although they undertook to police the region until the new state came into being. Their previous actions had alienated the Arabs. The new proposals, particularly in view of the plight of the Jews in continental Europe, now alienated Jewish communities in Palestine and elsewhere.

ISRAEL

The independent Palestine that Britain envisaged was never founded. At the close of the Second World War there was mounting pressure from the United States (where the American Jews were successful in organizing themselves politically) and from Jewish terrorists in Palestine for the British to relax their immigration policy. Weakened and impoverished by the war, Britain invited the United States to participate in a committee of enquiry into the post-war plight of the Jews. The committee recommended that Palestine immigration limitations be lifted. The British government hesitated. The Arabs, speaking through the newly-formed Arab League, rejected the report.

As a result of a vote by the United Nations General Assembly, the new state of Israel was proclaimed in May 1948. Note how close Tel Aviv is to the eastern border.

On 14 February 1947 the British Foreign Secretary announced that Arab objections prevented a partition of Palestine and the mandate could not be governed as it then stood. Consequently, he was handing over the Palestinian problem to the United Nations. On 21 August 1947 the majority of a UN committee of enquiry recommended that Palestine be divided along the lines suggested by the Peel Commission of 1936-7. The plan was accepted by the General Assembly of the UN on 29 November, carried by thirty-three votes to thirteen. The United States and the Soviet Union voted in favour, Britain against. The Jews adopted the Biblical name Israel for their new homeland.

The Arabs viewed this solution as the last straw

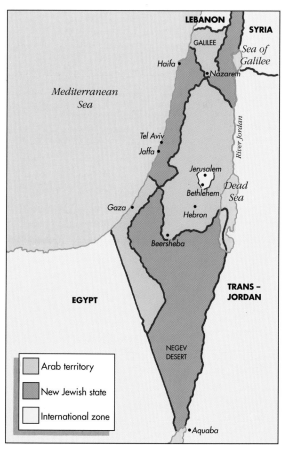

LEBANON
SYRIA
GALILEE
Sea of Galilee
Haifa
Nazareth
Mediterranean Sea
River Jordan
Tel Aviv
Jaffa
Jerusalem
Bethlehem
Dead Sea
Gaza
Hebron
Beersheba
TRANS – JORDAN
EGYPT
NEGEV DESERT

Arab territory

New Jewish state

International zone

Aquaba

Jewish refugees disembark at the port of Haifa in 1947 after their ship was intercepted by British destroyers. Jewish organizations in the United States and Palestine urged the British to relax their immigration policy in the period leading up to the creation of Israel.

It is the natural right of the Jewish people to lead, as do all other nations, an independent existence in their sovereign State.

Accordingly we, the members of the National Council representing the Jewish people in Palestine . . . hereby proclaim the establishment of the Jewish State in Palestine, to be called Medinath Yisrael (the State of Israel).

From the State of Israel Declaration of Independence, 14 May 1948.

in their struggle to make Palestine an independent Arab state. Not surprisingly, they rejected the idea of an imposed partition. As the future Palestinian leader Yasser Arafat was to claim: 'The Assembly [of the UN] partitioned what it had no right to divide — an indivisible homeland.'

In the months before partition dozens of Britons, Jews and Arabs were killed. As the British evacuated a town, Jews and Arabs fought to gain control over it. Thousands of Palestinian Arabs fled to neighbouring Arab states. By 1948 units from the regular armies of Egypt, Syria and Iraq were involved. When the state of Israel came into being in May 1948, it was simultaneously attacked by the armies of Lebanon, Syria, Iraq, Transjordan, Saudi Arabia and Egypt. The modern Arab-Israeli conflict had officially begun.

CONCLUSION

The causes of the Arab-Israeli conflict were deep-rooted and intractable. They included the rise of nationalism among both the Jewish and Arab peoples, misguided and contradictory British statements made during the First World War, uncertain government of the Palestinian mandate between the wars and the wave of sympathy for the Jewish cause which followed the horrific anti-Semitic policies of the Nazis. To these may be added Jewish insensitivity towards Arab fears, the unwillingness of the Arabs to compromise and the heavy-handed action of the United Nations in pressing ahead with partition in the face of Arab and British opposition.

Could the conflict have been prevented? No historical event is inevitable. Had courageous people from either side met, determined to solve the problem peaceably, a compromise might have been found. That is, after all, what eventually began to happen. But there were no such leaders at the time. And the longer the problem dragged on, the more deeply entrenched each side became. In the end, it took thirty years of bloodshed to even begin to move them.

Israel's first prime minister David Ben-Gurion (centre left, in jacket) watches as the last British troops leave from the port of Haifa in July 1948.

AND SO TO WAR

The frontiers of Israel in 1949 after the First Arab-Israeli War. The Israelis gained control over huge swathes of new territory, but the Arabs held on to the West Bank and recaptured part of Jerusalem.

The first and most obvious consequence of the Arab-Israeli conflict was war, and with war came death, destruction, homelessness and misery.

In a sense it is not strictly accurate to divide the military conflict between Arab and Israeli into separate wars, because no Arab state made peace with Israel until the Camp David agreement of 1978 formally ended hostilities between Egypt and Israel. Nevertheless, although there was a perpetual state of war from 1948 to 1978 (and beyond for most Arabs), the fighting flared into full-scale military conflict on only four occasions.

MAY 1948 — JULY 1949

When the Arab armies moved against Israel in 1948, most observers, including the Arabs themselves, expected the new state to be swept off the map in months, if not weeks. Surprisingly, this did not happen. Not only did the Israelis resist the invasion, they also managed to drive back their assailants and capture large areas of Palestine. 6,000 Israelis and many more Arabs were killed in the fighting.

Military historians now realize that Israeli success was not so surprising. The numbers of ground troops on either side were roughly similar. Although initially outgunned by their enemies, by 1949 the Israelis had managed to buy large quantities of modern arms and equipment from abroad. The Jewish army was formed around the well-established Haganah. Their troops were experienced and

Soldiers of the Israeli Haganah force on the way to Jerusalem, 1948. Every single member of the contingent was killed shortly after this picture had been taken.

knew the territory they were fighting in. Above all, they were fighting for survival. They had to win — if they did not, they and their families would be driven out of their new homeland.

The Arab forces, on the other hand, were divided into separate, inexperienced armies under their own commanders operating with different battle plans. These problems, which bedevilled the Arabs in all their wars with Israel, reflected more fundamental difficulties. As the old mandate powers withdrew from the region after the Second World War, deep divisions emerged within the Arab world about how the Middle East should be organized. There were essentially three very different visions of what the Middle East should look like politically. One vision was Pan-Arabism. This was the somewhat ill-defined notion, arising out of the struggle for independence from the old imperial and colonial powers, that all Arabs should be united in a brotherhood reminiscent of the great days of Arab power that began in the seventh century. It found its most positive expression in the Arab League formed in March 1945 by the governments of Egypt, Iraq, Lebanon, Saudi Arabia, Syria, Transjordan and Yemen. It was a loose association, intended to promote understanding and trade between the member states.

Pan-Arabism's principal difficulty was reconciliation with the second vision of regional order: emerging nationalism, fostered by the governments of the separate, mostly newly-independent Arab states. Understandably, member states tended to put their own interests before those of the wider group. The

Arabs made separate truces with Israel between January and July 1949. Furthermore, Transjordan (renamed Jordan in 1949) and Egypt annexed the Palestinian lands not occupied by Israel. The disappearance of the Palestinian state was, therefore, completed by the Arabs' own actions. During the fighting there was always a fear that one Arab state might outperform the others, thereby increasing its own power at the expense of its neighbours'. For example, the Arab League refused to recognize Jordan's annexation of the Palestinian land on the west bank of the River Jordan. One of the consequences of the Arab-Israeli conflict was to widen the divide between separate Arab nations, not close it.

The third force or vision running through the Arab world was Pan-Islamism, or the call for all Muslims to unite against the infidel. In theory, this was a powerful sentiment for the Arab leaders to harness. But it was a double-edged sword. In Lebanon, where the population was divided between Christian and Muslim, it was to pull the country apart. Another problem was that the more charismatic Islamic leaders tended to be suspicious of Western technology and opposed to all-powerful secular governments. This led them into conflict with governments like that of the Saud family of Saudi Arabia, where fundamentalists rioted at the opening of the first television transmission centre. Islamic fundamentalism's greatest triumph, bringing down the authoritarian, secular regime of the Shah of Iran in 1979, was a stern warning to all governments

Some of the 800,000 Arab refugees created by the war of 1948–9 receiving medical aid from the Red Cross at Jiziya.

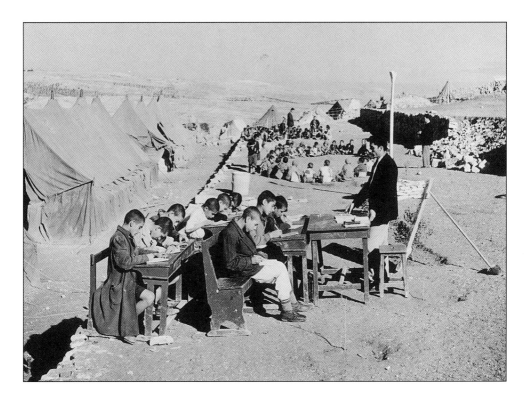

in the Middle East and beyond. The fundamentalist-moderate split divided the Palestinian Liberation Organization, which represented the Palestinian cause, and destabilized Arab states, such as Egypt.

THE CONSEQUENCES OF WAR

The beginning of years of exile and hardship — Palestinian refugee children at a makeshift school in a Jordanian camp, 1949.

The consequences of the First Arab-Israeli War set the agenda for the region for the rest of the century. It confirmed the existence of the state of Israel, although this was not recognized by the Arabs. Israel came into being with no fixed boundaries. The war expanded the territory under Israeli control by about a quarter. To the south-east it stretched to the port of Eilat on the Gulf of Aqaba. From here the frontier ran north to the Mediterranean, along the boundary of the old Palestinian mandate. At the coast Egypt took over the Gaza Strip. In the north Israel's frontier was divided from Syria by the Golan Heights. To the east a large enclave on the west bank of the River Jordan remained in Arab hands. These frontiers were guaranteed by Britain, France and the United States in 1950.

The war had serious consequences for Israel. Around 4,000 Jewish soldiers and 2,000 Jewish civilians were killed during this first war. It became a country on a permanent war footing, maintaining one of the world's largest armies in proportion to population and spending about twenty per cent of its wealth on the armed forces. Although assisted by substantial foreign investment and aid, disproportionate military spending prevented the economy from expanding as it might have done. Israel became a country under siege. Its citizens were subject to compulsory military service and grew up with a dour, siege mentality. Negotiations were frowned upon in case they were seen as signs of weakness, and hostility mounted towards all Arabs, both within and without their heavily defended frontiers.

If the consequences of the war were tough for Israel, they were even more so for millions of Palestinians. Thousands had been killed, both in the war and at the hands of Jewish terrorists. One of the worst massacres occurred in April 1948, when some 250 Arab men, women and children were killed in the village of Deir Yasin. The United Nations estimated that 750,000 Palestinians fled from Israeli rule during 1948-9. Some found new homes and work, but many settled in the vast refugee camps established along Israel's borders. Because of the strain these refugees put on local resources, they were not always welcome. Those who found jobs and worked hard also became objects of scorn among their fellow Arabs. 'The Jews of the Arab World' was one description given to them.

The Arabs left behind in Israel fared little better. Here they were second-class citizens in a country striving to promote its Jewishness. The Israelis declared that the Arabs within their frontiers had a higher standard of living than that enjoyed in many other Arab countries. However, this was scant consolation to a people who — like South African black people under apartheid — believed they were living in a land stolen from them by outsiders.

The war had consequences for the wider Arab world, too. It increased Arab suspicion of the United States, which had recognized the state of Israel the day it was formed. Defeat in the war of 1948-9 hastened the downfall of King Farouk of Egypt and the passage of power into the hands of fervent nationalists.

Finally, the most dangerous consequence of the First Arab-Israeli War was an Arab determination to seek revenge for their humiliation. Far from solving the problem of Palestine, the war had only made it worse.

The Palestine problem is the story of a people who lived peacefully in their own homes for generations. Then along came total strangers across the sea who turned the people out of their country and occupied their homes.

S Hadawi, an Arab writer, cited in Walter Oppenheim, *The Middle East,* Blackwell, 1989

PLAYERS IN A WIDER GAME

THE COLD WAR

During the Second World War the communist Soviet Union and democratic capitalist United States had fought together as uneasy allies. From 1943 onwards, when it was looking increasingly likely that the Axis powers (Nazi Germany, Italy and Japan) would be defeated, the Soviet and American governments started considering the post-war world. In conferences held at Yalta (February 1945) and Potsdam (June 1945) the two superpowers came to provisional agreements about each other's sphere of influence. This accord did not last. Neither side understood or trusted the other, and by 1947 they were at loggerheads. Both built up huge stockpiles of weapons and tried to outdo the other in attracting friends and allies around the world. The era of the Cold War had begun.

The 'Big Three' at the Yalta Conference, February 1945 — (left to right) Soviet Premier Joseph Stalin, United States President Franklin D Roosevelt and British Prime Minister Winston Churchill. Allied accord did not survive long after the war, and the Middle East became a central focus for the US-Soviet Cold War.

The Suez Canal in 1951, an essential link in the route that supplied oil from the Middle East to the West, When Nasser came to power in 1952 he was determined to reclaim the canal from the British, who maintained a military presence in the area.

Wherever there was conflict, the Soviets and the Americans watched carefully to see whether they might take advantage of the situation. The Arab-Israeli conflict drew their attention to the Middle East. To begin with they adopted similar positions, supporting the United Nations resolution calling for the partition of Palestine and the establishment of the state of Israel. American Jews sent funds to the Israelis, while the Soviets allowed Israel to purchase arms. In the 1950s, however, events in Egypt put an end to this understanding and set the superpowers against each other in the Middle East. Outside backing deepened and intensified the Arab-Israeli conflict, while also fuelling the hostility of the Cold War.

THE SECOND ARAB-ISRAELI WAR

The military coup that toppled the Egyptian monarchy in 1952 eventually brought to power Colonel Gamal Abdul Nasser (1918–1970). Nasser was a Pan-Arab nationalist. His aim was to free his country of foreigners (there were still British bases along the Suez Canal) and to lead the Arab world. To do this, he was prepared to play off the United States against the Soviet Union.

Before Nasser came to power, American policy in the Middle East had been quite successful. The United States had appeased the Arabs by refusing to sell arms to Israel; and also sponsored an anti-communist union, known as the Baghdad Pact, comprising Turkey, Pakistan, Iraq, Iran and Britain. Nasser refused to join the Pact. Instead, in September 1955 he came to an agreement with the Soviets to exchange cotton for Czechoslovakian arms. In the eyes of the world the Soviet Union was now seen as the defender of Arab nationalism against the West. The Cold War had come to the Middle East.

The United States tried to get Nasser back into its camp by offering $50 million to fund his massive Aswan Dam project on the River Nile. It also put pressure on him by agreeing to France selling NATO arms to Israel. When Nasser refused to play the Americans' game, they withdrew funding for the Aswan Dam in July 1956. In response, Nasser nationalized the Suez Canal, saying he would use its revenues to pay for the dam. The action made him an Arab hero. Shivers of consternation ran through the Western world — the canal was a vital route for the supply of oil from the Middle East.

Britain, France and Israel – but not the United States – decided to intervene. Tension had been mounting along the border between Egypt and Israel, and on 29 October the Israelis launched a full-scale attack. The next day, having secretly planned the operation with Israel beforehand, Britain and France attacked Egypt. First they bombed military targets, then they sent in

HANDS OFF EGYPT
In defiance of the UN charter and the principles of international law, the Anglo-French imperialists have launched an intervention against the independent Egyptian Republic in an attempt to seize by armed force the Suez Canal.

Report in the Soviet newspaper *Pravda*, 2 November 1956

Troops of the Anglo-French invasion force in Port Said, Egypt, in 1956. Without American backing, the European assault proved a costly embarrassment.

troops to seize the Suez Canal. Although Israel, Britain and France achieved their military objective, the Egyptians had blocked the canal before it was taken and it remained shut for many months.

For a few tense days, with the Soviet Union threatening to intervene unless the aggressors withdrew, it looked as if the conflict might expand into a global one. United States forces went on standby. Fortunately, the Soviet Union was taken up with an anti-communist revolt in Hungary, and the United States had sufficient economic power to force Britain and France to abide by a United Nations resolution and withdraw. The Israelis followed suit the following year.

Full-scale war had been averted. Britain and France had been humiliated and Arab morale boosted. But with the interference of the superpowers in the Middle East, the Arab-Israeli conflict had taken a turn for the worse. And the Palestinian problem was as far from a solution as it had ever been.

THE SOVIETS AND THE AMERICANS

For many years the Middle East remained one of the regions where East-West confrontation was at its most dangerous. The course of events was extremely

Scuttled ships block the Suez Canal, 1956. This move by the Egyptians rendered ineffective the Anglo-French seizure of the canal a short while later.

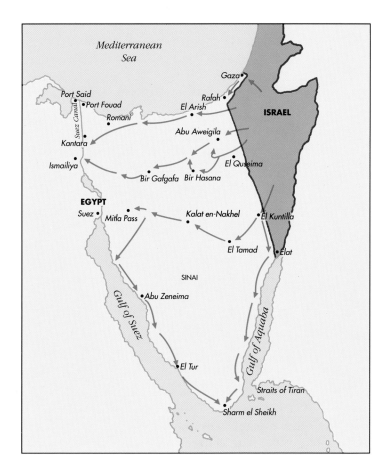

The lines of Israel's attack on Egypt which began on 29 October 1956. By 5 November Sinai was in Israeli hands. At the same time, British and French troops seized the Suez Canal.

complex, with a bewildering series of wars, coups and treaties following one another in quick succession. The Arabs were rarely united, and the activities of the superpowers (the United States and the Soviet Union) made a solution to the region's problems more difficult to achieve, at least until the later 1970s.

One destabilizing factor was the superpowers' diplomatic manoeuvring over the Middle East. In the 1960s, for example, the Soviet Union engaged in a massive anti-Zionist campaign among the Arabs. This was not done for reasons of principle, but to unite the Arabs against the United States' ally, Israel. It served only to increase tension in the area. It may also be argued that the Soviet Union precipitated the Third War (1967) by leaking a false warning to Egypt that its ally Syria was about to be attacked by Israel, and by telling the Egyptians that it would keep the United States in check if war broke out. The Soviet Union alone was not to blame. The Americans pursued their interests in the area just as ruthlessly. It is rumoured that the United States was behind the coups in Syria

Cold War spin-off — British troops examine Soviet-made rocket launchers captured from the Egyptians, 1956.

If there is indeed a danger of nuclear confrontation in the Middle East, it would be enormously increased by a guaranteed settlement, which would involve the guarantors [the United States and the Soviet Union] in every border incident.

Bernard Lewis, *The Great Powers, the Arabs and the Israelis*, New York, 1969

(1961) and Iraq (1963) that temporarily removed those countries from the Soviet sphere of influence.

The primary manner in which the United States and the Soviet Union fuelled the Arab-Israeli conflict was by supplying arms to either side. As we have seen, the process began in 1955 with Nasser's agreement to obtain arms from Czechoslovakia and the United States' response of agreeing to France supplying Israel. The year after the Suez crisis the United States Congress launched its 'Eisenhower Doctrine', promising arms to any Middle East power seeking to resist communism.

It has been estimated that between 1968 and 1973 the Soviet Union stocked the Arabs with arms worth $2,600 million, while over the same period the United States provided Israel with weapons worth about half that sum, as well as economic aid worth $420 million. By the end of 1970 there were 20,000 Soviet military advisors in Egypt. These were soon joined by Soviet pilots flying Egyptian aircraft. The weapons enabled Arabs and Israelis to engage in a Fourth Arab-Israeli War (1973). The weapons lost in this war were soon replaced, the Egyptians and Syrians reportedly receiving $4,000 million worth of Soviet arms in 1974, including Scud missiles. Sources say that in the same year the Israelis bought arms from the United States to the value of $1,500 million. A refusal to provide arms to Israel and the Arabs (if such a move had been feasible) would not have solved the Palestinian question, but it might have made both sides less ready to resort to war.

Another consequence of US-Soviet involvement in the Arab-Israeli conflict was that on occasion it brought the world close to nuclear disaster. In 1967 the Soviet Union said it would intervene militarily in the war, even launching rockets against Britain and France, unless the Israeli advance was stopped. There was a similar crisis over Jordan in 1970 and again during the Fourth War (1973), when all Soviet airborne divisions were held on standby and the American armed forces put on global alert. Only last-minute compromise prevented the Arab-Israeli conflict from having the most horrific consequence of all.

President Nasser of Egypt (centre) with Soviet leader Nikita Khrushchev (left) and President Tito of Yugoslavia (right) in 1960. The supply of arms from the Soviet Union and the United States enabled Arabs and Israelis to continue in their bitter fight for Palestine.

WAR AND OIL

THE CONSEQUENCES OF THE SECOND ARAB-ISRAELI WAR

Moshe Dayan (1915–81), Israeli chief of staff in the Sinai War of 1956 and Minister of Defence during the Six-Day War of 1967. He is seen here with General Ariel Sharon, who became Minister of Defence some years later.

The Second Arab-Israeli War, also known as the Suez-Sinai Campaign, changed the focus of the Middle East. The two superpowers, the United States and the Soviet Union, were now major players in the region. In 1956 both governments put their forces on alert, ready to intervene if events took a turn they found unacceptable.

The expansion of American and Soviet influence in the region was at the expense of Britain and France. Following the ill-advised Suez campaign and ignominious withdrawal of British forces, British

Prime Minister Anthony Eden resigned in 1957. The humiliation also helped bring about the collapse of France's Fourth Republic the following year. Furthermore, Britain and France's overseas colonies took advantage of their masters' imperial weakness and pressed harder for independence.

Interestingly, President Nasser emerged from the war stronger than ever. He dismissed his side's military setbacks. Egypt, he claimed, had tackled Britain, France and Israel, held the Suez Canal, and forced its enemies to withdraw. A United Nations force (UNEF) now guarded his Sinai frontier and Gamal Abdul Nasser was undisputed leader of the Arab world. His position was strengthened in 1958 when Egypt and Sinai joined together to form the United Arab Republic, which lasted until the Syrian coup of 1961. In Iraq the pro-British government was toppled, also in 1958, and the new regime was rewarded with Soviet weapons and aid.

Israel too had benefited from the conflict. It had once again proved its military proficiency and maintained its outlet to the Red Sea via the port of Eilat. UNEF provided a degree of protection against guerrilla attacks from Egypt. Sadly, of course, a conflict that left both Egypt and Israel feeling stronger and more confident was unlikely to bring the Arab-Israeli conflict any closer to a resolution.

THE SIX-DAY WAR

A third Arab-Israeli War, commonly known as the Six-Day War, broke out in June 1967. Its causes have long been a source of disagreement among politicians and historians. Its immediate cause was a massive pre-emptive air strike launched by the Israelis against their Arab neighbours on 5 June. By then, however, war was all but inevitable.

What had brought the two sides, neither of whom seemed to want war, to this position? Most obviously, the Arabs still refused to accept Israel's right to exist, while the Israeli government would not recognize how their country had been created at the expense of the Palestinian Arabs. Since the 1956 war, Palestinian nationalist movements had strengthened considerably, further destabilizing the region (see Chapter Nine). Furthermore, aid from the two superpowers had modernized and increased the size of both Israeli and Arab armed forces.

Israeli forces advance through Sinai as Egyptian prisoners are taken away by truck in the opposite direction, 1967.

The tension mounted in 1966 with armed clashes between Israeli and Syrian and Jordanian forces, and an Egyptian-Syrian defence pact. In 1967 the situation spiralled out of control, fuelled by a false Soviet intelligence report that Israel was planning to attack Syria. Nasser moved in Sinai, UNEF withdrew, and Egyptian forces cut Israel's access to the Red Sea.

Israel's new Defence Minister, Moshe Dayan, believed he had no choice but to attack. Within hours the Israeli air force had destroyed 385 Egyptian, Syrian and Jordanian aircraft, mostly on the ground. With complete command of the air, Israel had an enormous strategic advantage. Within three days its forces had reached the Suez Canal. In the east, they drove the Jordanians back over the Jordan River, and by 9 June they were over the Golan Heights and on the road to Damascus, the capital of Syria. King Hussein of Jordan surrendered on 6 June and Egypt and Syria followed four days later.

As with previous conflicts, the Six Day War brought the Palestinian problem no closer to a peaceful resolution. Some 15,000 military personnel, mostly Arabs, had died. Israel's frontiers had expanded dramatically (see map on p.46) and, along the Gaza Strip and in the West Bank, it governed some 665,000 more Palestinians. The Arabs and their Soviet backers had been humiliated, and henceforward co-operation between the Arab states declined. The American belief that Israel was its prime ally in the region had been emphatically confirmed.

Unlikely as it seemed however, Israel's triumph contained the seeds of a resolution to the Arab-Israeli conflict. After hours of discussion, the United Nations Security Council agreed Resolution 242. This stated, first, that it was illegal to seize territory by war; second, that each nation in the region had the right to live in peace within secure boundaries; third, that the Middle East problem should be solved by Israel exchanging conquered land for permanent peace; and, fourth, that peace involved a just settlement of the problem of the Palestinian refugees, 400,000 more of whom had been created by the war.

Here at last was a basis for negotiation between Arabs and Israelis. Unexpectedly, Resolution 242 also succeeded in bringing the conflict to a new phase. Gradually, over the next fifteen years, it began to shift the world's focus from the Arab-Israeli con-

The reality of war — a wounded Egyptian prisoner of war, stripped of his uniform, is supported by his comrades, 1967.

We will win because we must live. Our neighbours are fighting not for their lives, nor for their sovereignty. They are fighting to destroy us. We dare not be destroyed.

From a speech by Israel's Prime Minister, Golda Meir, 13 October 1973

The battlefields of the remarkable Six-Day War of 1967, when Israel captured Sinai and the key strategic areas of the Golan Heights and the West Bank.

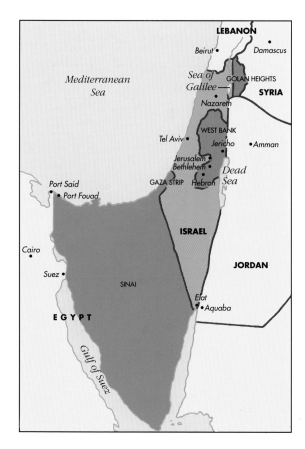

flict to just one aspect of that problem: the question of Palestine.

THE OIL WEAPON

Nasser's successor, Anwar Sadat (1918-81) wanted a permanent peace with Israel. He knew that this could not be achieved by force. Nevertheless, placing Egyptian and Syrian forces under his joint control in January 1973, he actively pursued a war that would raise Egypt's prestige in future negotiations. This was the Fourth Arab-Israeli War of October 1973.

Launching a surprise attack on 6 October, the Jewish holy day of Yom Kippur, Egyptian and Syrian forces met with early success and brought Israel close to defeat. Nevertheless, assisted by substantial American aid, Israel regrouped and was once again striking deep into Egyptian and Syrian territory when the United States and Soviet Union arranged a cease-fire on 22 October. The Soviets had been prepared to go to Egypt's aid if the fighting had continued for much longer.

The war permanently changed the Middle East situation. First, the Arabs had shown that they could hurt Israel – and would continue to do so until a settlement was reached. Second, they showed that they could hurt the rest of the world, too. In October 1973, to help Arab armies in the field, the Arab-dominated Organisation of Oil Exporting Countries (OPEC) agreed to double the price of oil, cut production and cease exports to countries directly supporting Israel. Since over half the world's oil came from the Arab oil fields and these provided western nations with most of their supplies, the effect was immediately devastating.

Fuel prices rocketed, industry slumped and inflation soared. America, Israel's

An Israeli soldier tends a wounded comrade during the Yom Kippur War of October 1973.

most powerful ally and engine of the world economy, was hardest hit. Its motor industry, proud manufacturers of 'gas-guzzling' limousines, was rocked by cheaper foreign car imports. Europe was hit almost as hard.

Against this troubled background, years of peace negotiations began, brokered by the United States. They eventually led to United States President Jimmy Carter persuading Israeli Prime Minister Menachem Begin (1913-92) and Egyptian President Anwar Sadat to sign an historic peace settlement in Washington DC on 17 September 1978. This became known as the famous Camp David agreements. On the basis of peace in exchange for land, the first part said Israel would hand back the region of Sinai to Egypt, in return for a peace treaty and full normal relations between the two countries. This was implemented. The second part, which stated that Israel would hand over to the Palestinians the land it had occupied since 1967 – the Gaza Strip and the West Bank of the River Jordan – was a non-starter.

The agreement shattered Arab unity. Israelis were also divided between Begin's supporters and those who believed he had sacrificed his country's security. Finally, many Palestinians were now convinced that they could not rely on the support of Arab neighbours. Their fate, they decided, lay in their own hands.

We have fought for the sake of peace, the only peace that really deserves to be called peace — peace based on justice. Our enemy sometimes speaks about peace. But there is a vast difference between the peace of aggression and the peace of justice.

President Sadat of Egypt in a speech to the People's Assembly, Cairo, 16 October 1973

THE PALESTINIANS

THE PEOPLE NOBODY WANTED

Seeking a new home: aged Palestinian refugees trudge across the River Jordan, 1947.

S ince 1948, the sufferings of the Palestinians have been almost unending. Most obviously, they lost out as a consequence of the creation of Israel. This was directly contrary to the recommendation of the United Nations Special Committee for Palestine (UNSCOP) that the former British mandate (see page 27) be partitioned between Jews and Arabs, with the holy city of Jerusalem under international control.

The formation of Israel left the Palestinian Arabs with no immediate hope of establishing a state

of their own. By early 1949 150,000 of them lived in Israel. A further 450,000 were in Transjordan (Jordan) and 200,000 in Egypt. Perhaps 700,000 more were stateless, homeless refugees scattered throughout the Middle East or gathered in emergency relief camps established by the United Nations.

Although in 1948 their fellow Arabs in the Arab League talked of solidarity with the Palestinians and their determination to oppose the creation of a Jewish state in the Middle East, the reality was very different. Both Transjordan and Egypt gained Palestinian-inhabited territory during the First Arab-Israeli War, thereby extending their own frontiers. This tendency to put national interests before those of the Arabs as a whole continued as long as the conflict itself. It manifested itself, for example, in Jordan's expulsion of the Palestine Liberation Organisation (see page 54) and Egypt's independent peace with Israel (see page 47).

The Six-Day War, in which Israel seized the West Bank and the Gaza Strip, brought a further

Old site, new owners: Israeli soldiers celebrate their capture in the 1967 war of the Dome of the Rock, a site sacred to all Muslims.

900,000 Palestinian Arabs under Israeli rule in 1967. Israel now contained about three million Jews and 1.2 million Arabs. A further three million Palestinians lived in Jordan, the Gulf States, Lebanon, Syria, Saudi Arabia and elsewhere.

About a quarter of all Palestinians, over a million people, lived in UN refugee camps established in Lebanon, Israel (including the West Bank and Gaza Strip), Syria and Jordan. Living conditions in these camps were very poor indeed. Men, women and children, crowded together in faded tents and ramshackle huts of tin and concrete, lived off scant water supplies and United Nations rations. Education facilities and employment prospects were at best very limited. As well as appalling living conditions, camp dwellers endured violence and intimidation from Palestinian militants, other Arab groups, and Israeli forces. Not surprisingly, after visiting the West Bank camps in 1988, one leading Western politician described them simply as 'hell'.

No way to live: a homeless Palestinian makes the best use he can of scarce water supplies in a UN refugee camp, 1967. The plight of the Palestinians shocked many who had previously supported Israel in its struggle for survival.

The soldiers of tomorrow - Palestinian children of the al-Fatah movement being trained in the art of war.

Only the United Nations accepted responsibility for Palestinian refugees. The Arabs pointed out, quite accurately, that they were the product of Israeli conquest and therefore Israel's responsibility. The Israelis responded, also with some justification, that the Arabs allowed the terrible conditions in the camps to persist for political reasons, to evoke sympathy for their cause. One day's oil revenues, Israelis pointed out, could solve the problem overnight. Moreover, they claimed that the camps were a recruiting ground for Palestinian terrorists and were even used as terrorist bases (see pages 57-9).

A PALESTINIAN NATION

An obvious consequence of the formation of the state of Israel was the creation of an Israeli nation. Ironically, this was paralleled by the emergence of a Palestinian nation. Before 1948 the Jews were a people without a homeland; afterwards it was the Palestinians who were in that position – and they wanted the situation redressed urgently.

As there had never previously been a independent state called 'Palestine', Palestinian nationalism emerged slowly. At first the Palestinian Arabs had no coherent organization. The world viewed their ineffective leader, the Mufti of Jerusalem, with great suspicion as he had lived in Nazi Germany during the Second World War. Furthermore, his role as both a religious (Muslim) and secular leader was ill-suited to the post-war world.

In 1949 the Mufti established himself in Gaza at the head of an 'All-Palestine Government' and encouraged groups of young Arab men to wage a terrorist war against the new state of Israel. During the 1950s these groups, known as *fedayeen* (fanatics), attacked mainly military targets from bases outside Israel's borders. The groups were not specifically religious in character and operated in a rather haphazard manner.

By the mid-1950s, a number of Palestinian militants had realized that the Arab states bordering Israel were not unduly concerned with the plight of the stateless Palestinians. Tired of the Mufti's weak leadership, a group of them met in Kuwait and formed an independent organization – *Fatah* (Victory) – with the aim of co-ordinating anti-Israeli activity. Among Fatah's leaders was a man who would play a key role in Palestinian affairs for the rest of the century – Yasser Arafat.

The Grand Mufti of Jerusalem with Adolf Hitler. Although he lived in Nazi Germany from 1942–5, the Mufti continued to exercise influence in the Middle East both during and after the Second World War.

Independent Palestinian activity worried Arab governments. Consequently, in 1964, Nasser encouraged the formation of the Palestine Liberation Organization (PLO). This organization, which Nasser hoped to dominate, would co-ordinate all Palestinian efforts to create a 'democratic and secular Palestine' and bring about the 'elimination' of Israel. Its structure was based on the political Palestine National Council (PNC) and the military Palestine Liberation Army (PLA). In fact, the PLO did not increase Nasser's control over Palestinian activity, but it did play a key role in fostering the idea of a Palestinian nation.

Palestinians, living in poverty and often discriminated against by both Arabs and Israelis, were understandably attracted to the PLO. It represented their hopes and ambitions. It soon sprouted more terrorist groups, like the Popular Front for the Liberation of Palestine (PFLP) and the Democratic Front for the Liberation of Palestine (DFLP). Presiding over all of them, although not always in firm control, was the PLO's chairman Yasser Arafat (first elected in 1969).

No one is safe. The wrecked interior of the Israeli school bus in which eight children and three adults were killed in a Palestinian bazooka attack, May 1970.

Al-Fatah, the largest and most moderate of the Palestinian resistance organizations, announced today that it was responsible for the guerrilla raid that resulted in seven deaths last night at the Israeli town of Nahariya.

The New York Times, 26 June 1974

TERROR TACTICS

By 1969, tough Israeli tactics had driven the PLO from the West Bank into Jordan. Here it came up against the moderate King Hussein, who was unwilling to stir up further trouble with Israel. By September 1970 the two sides were in open conflict and within a year the PLO had been driven from Jordan.

Now based in Beirut, Lebanon, the PLO continued to grow in stature and authority. In October 1974 a meeting of Arab governments in Rabat formally gave the PLO responsibility for all Palestinians. In the same year, the organization was recognized by the United Nations, when it was allowed to speak out on the problem of the disputed West Bank. Recognition by other governments soon followed. But the crucial recognition – Israel's – was still far off, hampering attempts at Arab-Israeli talks on a settlement of the Palestinian problem.

Meanwhile, backed by Arab money (especially from Saudi Arabia and Libya), the PLO continued its attacks. Targets were now more random. In 1976, for example, terrorist bombs killed eight Israelis in Jerusalem, and on 11 March 1978 a Palestinian war band landed on the coast north of Tel Aviv, hijacked a holiday bus and killed 39 Israelis.

Even more shocking, particularly as far as international opinion was concerned, were attacks on civilians outside Israel. These were generally made by extremist splinter groups of the PLO, such as Black September. Planes and airports were primary targets. In September 1970, for instance, the PLO hijacked four airliners, held 600 passengers hostage and destroyed three planes on the ground in Jordan. Two years later, five Black September terrorists and eleven Israeli athletes died in a raid on the Munich Olympic Games.

Most observers argued that such terrorist activity was morally abhorrent and harmed the Palestinian cause by alienating world opinion. In response, the terrorists said that they were at war with Israel and in war any tactics were justified. If the innocent were harmed, they claimed, the fault lay with the Israelis for the greatest terrorist act of all – the seizure of Palestine. Whether these arguments were valid or not, terrorist activity certainly kept the Palestinian issue in the headlines.

These criminal acts of hijacking planes, of detaining passengers, of blowing up aircraft are deplorable and must be condemned. It is high time we adopted effective measures to put a stop to this retreat to the law of the jungle.

The Secretary-General of the United Nations, cited in Walter Oppenheim, *The Middle East*, 1989

SEEKING SOLUTIONS

RIPPLES OF INSTABILITY

Perhaps some of the most dangerous repercussions of the Arab-Israeli conflict were upon the continuing United States-Soviet Cold War. The 1970 crisis between the Jordanian government of King Hussein and the militant Palestinians living within his kingdom is a telling example. In September 1970, frustrated by what he saw as a Palestinian 'state within a state' in Jordan, Hussein sent his army in against the PLO. The subsequent arrival of tanks from Syria, a friend of the Soviet Union and ally of the PLO, escalated the fighting into an international crisis. If Jordan fell to the PLO-Syrians, Israel would be surrounded by countries within the Soviet sphere of influence.

In response the United States put its armed forces on alert, ready to intervene on the side of the

The conflict spreads: smoke billows over Amman, Jordan, during the civil war fought between the Jordanian army of King Hussein and Palestinian guerillas, September 1970.

Jordanians if they were unable to halt the Syrians on their own. Although the Soviets urged Syria to show restraint, they too were unwilling to bend to American pressure. Fortunately, the Jordanian army managed to repel the Syrian attack and the Palestinians were driven from Jordan. Nevertheless, a major East-West conflict had only narrowly been averted.

The consequences of conflict showed within Israel, too. From 1948 to 1977 the country was dominated by the socialist-leaning Labour Party, led by Prime Ministers Ben-Gurion (1948-53 and 1955-63), Eshkol (1963-69), Meir (1969-74) and Rabin (1974-77). However, by the end of the 1960s, the strain of living in a state of siege had begun to undermine Labour's power. In 1977 the Likud, a right-wing alliance backed by fervent Zionists, came to power under Prime Minister Begin (1977-83). Begin's government allowed Zionist settlers to move into the West Bank and onto the Golan Heights. This infuriated the Palestinians and made settlement of the Israeli-Palestinian question even less likely.

A Labour-Likud national coalition under Peres (1984-86) then Shamir (1986-92) reflected the way the country was divided. One side, Labour, was willing to

Russian-born Golda Meir (1898–1978) came to Palestine in 1921. She was Prime Minister of Israel from 1969–74, and is seen here with US Secretary of State Henry Kissinger and Mrs Kissinger near the end of her period of office.

negotiate a settlement with the Palestinians; the other, typified by Shamir, was reluctant to even recognize the PLO's existence.

THE MISERY OF LEBANON

Outside Israel, no country has felt the consequences of the Arab-Israeli conflict more heavily than Lebanon. With a delicate balance of Christian and Muslim populations, it was the state most likely to be destabilized by events to the south. Yet for many years, despite its border with Israel, it managed to remain comparatively unscathed. By the time of the last war, though, the situation was changing fast.

Lebanon was drawn into the Arab-Israeli struggle through the arrival of the PLO after its expulsion from Jordan in 1970-1. This proved to be the decisive trigger to an internal conflict. The Christians, generally backed by Israel, split into moderate and militant factions. The Muslims, supported by Israel's enemies, became even more divided, both by sect and politics. All groups were funded and supplied with weapons by outsiders, among whom Libya now featured prominently. The situation was further troubled by Syrian and Israeli invasions of Lebanon. Large areas of the prosperous city of Beirut – once the 'Paris of the Middle East' – were smashed and burned.

A Shi'ite militia man fires a deadly rocket-propelled grenade at Palestinians in the Sabra refugee camp, Lebanon. The spread of the Arab-Israeli conflict into the volatile cultural mix of modern Lebanon was one of the conflict's more tragic consequences.

Rescuers search through the remains of the bombed head-quarters of the United States marines, Beirut, October 1983.

Lebanese and Palestinian refugees were starved, shot at and shelled.

The civil war began in Lebanon in 1975, following the massacre of Palestinian bus passengers. Syria sent in troops the following year and the Israelis in 1978. UN peacekeeping efforts failed, and Israel invaded a second time in 1982, forcing the PLO from the country to a new base in Tunisia. The next month a pro-Israeli Lebanese Christian faction carried out a terrible massacre in the Chabra and Chatila refugee camps, close to Beirut. The Israelis controlling the area, who had done nothing to stop the killing of an estimated 2,000 men, women and children, stood condemned. A UN multi-national peace force failed to hold the warring sides apart and pulled out shortly after a suicide bomber blew up an United States marine base, killing 241 people.

The situation in Lebanon deteriorated into a nightmare of fighting and hostage taking, with the Syrians and Israelis intervening from time to time to support their own interests. After the withdrawal of the PLO, extreme Islamic groups, such as *Hezbollah* ('Party of God', set up in 1982), moved to the front line in the campaign against Israel.

Two developments finally ended the tragedy. One was the collapse of the Soviet Union, softening the Middle East divisions it had engendered. The other was the Taif Accord, a peace plan prepared by the Arab League in October 1989. By 1990 a shaky peace had returned to Lebanon and its citizens began the painstaking task of rebuilding their broken land. The last Israeli troops left in 2000.

INTIFADA

Such was the dangerous instability created by the Arab-Israeli conflict that powerful outsiders – notably the United Nations and the United States – frequently tried to broker a solution to the problem. They met with little success before the lengthy discussions following the Fourth War in which the Soviet leadership, judging that peace, even when negotiated by their enemy, was better than war, stood aside. The talks eventually bore fruit in the historic Israel-Egypt Camp David settlement of 1978.

The signing of the Camp David Agreement, March 1979. Brokered by President Carter (centre), the accord between Egypt's President Anwar Sadat (left) and Israeli Prime Minister Mena-chem Begin (right) finally broke the Middle East stale-mate. Two years later Sadat was assassinated by Arab extremists.

Female supporters of the Shi'ite militia group Hezbollah demonstrate on the streets of Beirut by holding pictures of the Ayatallah Khomeini, leader of the Islamic revolution in Iran in 1979.

'During the past nine weeks, we have, in effect, destroyed the combat potential of 20,000 [PLO] terrorists. We hold 9,000 in a prison camp. Between 2,000 and 3,000 were killed and between 7,000 and 9,000 have been captured and cut off in Beirut. They have decided to leave there only because they have no possibility of remaining there. The problem will be solved.'

From a speech by Prime Minister Begin, 8 August 1982

The other Arab leaders condemned Sadat as a traitor for his role in the settlement and expelled Egypt from the Arab League. In October 1981, when Sadat was assassinated by Muslim extremists, the Arab-Israeli conflict had claimed one of its bravest victims. Nevertheless, Camp David had marked a significant turning point in the conflict. It added to the isolation of Yasser Arafat's PLO, soon to be expelled from Lebanon. The organization's authority and appeal was also threatened by more extreme religious groups like Hezbollah and later Hamas (the Islamic Resistance Movement), whose heady fanaticism appealed to angry young Palestinians.

Isolated in Tunisia, Arafat changed tactics. Thirty years of terrorism had failed – Israel was vastly larger and better defended than in 1948, and it was expanding its settlements into Palestinian areas, especially the West Bank. Arafat responded with diplomacy, talking to the United States, Jordan and even Egypt. He suggested that the Arabs might recognize Israel's right to exist if it returned to its pre-1967 frontiers. Then surely a Palestinian state might be created, perhaps in conjunction with Jordan?

Israel rejected such overtures. To hand back land, Prime Minister Shamir believed, would be a surrender – a betrayal of the thousands of Israelis who had died and been maimed in the conflict. By now 81 per cent of the West Bank's water supplies were being diverted to Israeli farms and settlements. Feeling isolated, neglected and betrayed by futile negotiations, in December 1987 the ordinary Palestinians living under Israeli rule had had enough. Taking matters into their own hands, they declared a spontaneous *Intifada* ('Shaking Off') against their Israeli oppressors.

Beginning in the Gaza Strip and spreading to the West Bank, the Intifada started with stone-throwing at Israeli police and security forces. Before long it escalated to guns and bombs. The Israeli authorities were uncertain how to react. Their soldiers were trained in warfare, not riot control. On occasion – often in full view of the world's media – they overreacted, using tear gas, rubber bullets and live ammunition on the trouble makers. Since the victims of these strong-arms tactics were often just young boys, international opinion was outraged. By 1991 the IDF (Israeli Defence Force) had killed 697 Arabs, seventy-eight of whom were under the age of fourteen. Thirteen Israeli security personnel had been killed, and a further dozen Israeli civilians had also died.

Recognizing how the Intifada had won international sympathy for the Palestinian cause, in late 1988 Yasser Arafat declared Palestine an independent state. Then, contrary to all previous pronouncements, he recognized the existence of Israel and rejected all forms of terrorism. On this basis, the United States said it

Palestinian youths express their people's frustration and anger at decades of ill-treatment by bombarding Israeli soldiers with rocks, 1988.

'Palestinians felt that they had reached a dead end: they were not living as free human beings and they had no hope for the future. The PLO was too fragmented and distant, the Arab states had lost interest. Europe and the Soviet Union lacked leverage and the US was too committed to Israel to comprehend the Palestinian situation, much less broker a satisfactory accord.'

Ann Mosley Lesch, 'The Palestinian Uprising: Causes and Consequences,' in *United Field Staff International Reports, Asia*, No. 1 (1988-89), p. 4

would talk with the PLO. Israel's conservative leader Yitzhak Shamir, however, still refused to negotiate.

Arafat's initiative was undone by the invasion of Kuwait by Iraq's Saddam Hussein in August 1990. The PLO, together with Libya, Sudan, Jordan and Yemen, refused to condemn the act of aggression. The next year, as a US-led coalition liberated Kuwait, Arab funds for the PLO dried up. Furthermore, respect for Israel rose when it refused to respond to Iraqi missile attacks. Delighted Palestinian cheering of these assaults did little to help their cause.

Enter the West: victorious US soldiers salute the flag outside their embassy in Kuwait after the withdrawal of Iraqi invasion forces, February 1991.

STRUGGLING TOWARDS SETTLEMENT

THE UNITED NATIONS FALLS SHORT

As one of the original supporters of the establishment of a Jewish state in Palestine, the United Nations was partly responsible for the region's subsequent troubles. Understandably, it was continually involved in trying to settle the situation amicably. Not one of its efforts met with much success. A decline in the UN's credibility as a peacekeeping organisation, therefore, must be listed as one of the less happy consequences of the Arab-Israeli conflict.

In 1948 the UN appointed a mediator to help Palestine adjust to independence. He was not able to

Inside a barrack room in the Mia Mia camp, Lebanon, 1952. The camp was funded by the United Nations Relief and Works Agency for Palestinian Refugees. Unable to stop the violence, the UN concentrated its efforts on helping the conflict's victims.

stop the fighting, but he did help supervise the truce demanded by the Security Council. Despite this, the UN's limitations became increasingly apparent as the conflict continued. Powerless to prevent the fighting in 1956, it arranged for the Suez Canal to be cleared, and sent its first peacekeeping force to hold the line between the opposing armies. The United Nations Emergency Force (UNEF) was deployed on Egyptian territory, with Egyptian consent. But when the Egyptians demanded UNEF's withdrawal in May 1967, the UN was forced to comply, leaving the way open for the Third Arab-Israeli War.

The UN reacted to the new outbreak of hostilities by calling for a cease-fire and then monitoring it. Although the disengagement and subsequent settlement between Israel and Egypt after the 1973 war was largely brokered by US diplomacy, the UN proved a useful neutral fourth party and provided the forces required to police Israel's borders with Egypt and Syria. UN's peacekeeping efforts in Lebanon proved less successful however. A pattern of the UN's involvement in the conflict soon emerged: an outbreak of violence – UN demands for a cease-fire and withdrawal – disengagement and arrival of UN observers and peace keepers – UN withdrawal when requested or threatened – a fresh outbreak of violence. The UN can resist aggression with armed force only with the unanimous support of members of the UN Security Council, as during the 1990-1 Gulf War. It has never found such unanimity over the Arab-Israeli conflict.

The Arabs were more successful than their Israeli counterparts at using the UN for propaganda purposes. Their chief coup was getting the Security Council to endorse UN Resolution 242 (see page 45) in 1967, which called for the withdrawal of

Man's best friend: Toffa, a German Shepherd dog working with the UN Emergency Force in Sinai, sits behind some of the mines she has sniffed out.

Israeli troops from all territories occupied that year. From 1974 the PLO was accepted as an observer at UN meetings. The next year the General Assembly set up a grandiose-sounding 'United Nations Committee on the Exercise of the Inalienable Rights of the Palestinian People'. Its demands, and similar ones by other UN bodies, carried little weight with the Security Council however and remained largely rhetoric. Even after 1993, when real progress was made towards a Middle East settlement, the UN's function was as a supporter, not an initiator.

In one area – work for the care of Palestinian refugees – the UN won the respect of all parties. When no one else would take responsibility for them, the UN set up the United Nations Relief and Works Agency for Palestine Refugees in the Near East (UNRWA). Since 1949, UNRWA has provided education, training, health and relief services to millions of Palestinian refugees. By 2000 it was helping some 3.7 million Palestinian refugees, running 647 refugee schools, eight vocational training centres and 122 health centres in 59 camps.

Palestinian recognition, 1974. Yasser Arafat addresses the UN General Assembly, from which the Israeli delegation (front row) was conspicuously absent.

THE ROAD MAP AND BEYOND

As Israel's Minister of Defence from 1984-90, the task of quashing the Intifada fell to the leading Labour politician Yitzhak Rabin (1922-95). By the end of his

Palestine's hope and future: Students in a Palestinian school in Ouza, 1993.

term in office, during which he had endorsed harsh repression, Rabin was convinced that force could not bring peace. There had to be discussion and compromise from both sides.

This conclusion coincided with the end of the Cold War, enabling the United States to concentrate more fully on the Middle East problem. Now Israel's enemies were not backed by the Soviets, the United States could put pressure on Israel to compromise by threatening to reduce the amount of aid it received.

In July 1992 Rabin became Prime Minister of Israel. Secret PLO-Israel talks were held in Oslo, Norway, that led to a breakthrough: a 'Declaration of Principles' involving mutual recognition and agreement on some steps towards a lasting settlement. Over the next year Israel began pulling its forces out of the Gaza Strip and the West Bank, and in 1996 Yasser Arafat was elected president of a Palestinian National Authority – a big step towards Palestinian autonomy. Israel and Jordan had finally made a formal peace two years earlier.

Tragically, one of the consequences of fifty years of conflict was the growth of extremist groups on either side. Muslim groups like Hamas and Islamic Jihad (Islamic Holy War) condemned the PLO's negotiations and stepped up terrorist attacks inside Israel.

For their part, passionate Zionists felt betrayed by Israel's new stance and vowed to oppose it. On 4 November 1995, Yigal Amir, a law student and fervent Zionist, shot and killed Rabin in cold blood. Benjamin Netanyahu, elected Israel's new Prime Minister in 1996 as terrorism mounted, pledged to make no further concessions to the Palestinians.

Efforts were made to re-start the peace process and several promising beginnings were made, but they foundered time and again on the unbending opposition of both side's extremists. Eventually, as tension mounted and hopes of progress dwindled, in the autumn of 2000 the Palestinians launched a second Intifada. The reaction in Israel was to elect the veteran hard-liner Ariel Sharon as the new Prime Minister.

Riots and terrorist bombings, often by young suicide attackers who believed they would go straight to heaven as martyrs to their cause, continued to make everyday life in Israel both restricted and dangerous. The Israelis responded with tougher and tougher action, re-entering the Gaza Strip and West Bank, attacking suspected terrorist bases with rocket-firing helicopters, and even imprisoning Arafat within his own headquarters in Gaza City.

The 11 September 2001 attack on New York by Osama Bin Laden's Al-Qaeda increased US sympathy for Israel in its fight against militant Islam. Moreover, President George W. Bush believed that ending Palestinian terrorism would help the USA's 'War Against Terror'. Therefore, after driving Al-Qaeda from Afghanistan and destroying the Saddam Hussein regime in Iraq, in 2003 the United States gave serious support to the 'road map', a multi-national plan for

'The Government and State of Israel and the P.L.O. team … (the Palestinian Delegation), representing the Palestinian people, agree that it is time to put an end to decades of confrontation and conflict, recognize their mutual legitimate and political rights, and strive to live in peaceful coexistence and mutual dignity and security and achieve a just, lasting and comprehensive peace settlement and historical reconciliation through the agreed political process.'

The Oslo Agreement, 13 September, 1993 [Cited in Walter Laquer and Barry Rubin, eds., *The Arab-Israeli Reader*, Penguin, 2001, p. 413.]

The cruel price of peace: Israelis mourn at the grave of their assassinated Prime Minister Yitzhak Rabin, November 1995.

67

'What can a man do when injustice becomes heavy and he finds none to ward it off from him? In that case he is forced into legiti-mate defence of soul, honor and land ... [Suicide bombers] are in a state of legitimate self-defence against those who attack them and do not show mercy to old people, children, or women...'

Sheikh Muhammed Sayyed Tantawi, 1997, head of Al-Azhar Islamic University, Cairo. [Cited in Barry Rubin and Judith Colp Rubin, *Anti-American Terrorism and the Middle East. A Documentary Reader. Understanding the Violence*, OUP, 2002, p. 36.]

peace between Israel and the Palestinians.

At first, the road map appeared to be leading somewhere. By early 2004, however, optimism was fading fast. Ariel Sharon's government infuriated Palestinian opinion by pressing ahead with a massive 'security fence' along a self-proclaimed eastern border. Arabs living in the West Bank said the wall deprived them of work, land and water. The Sharon government was also unwilling to dismantle Israeli settlements on West Bank land occupied in the 1967 war, although it did offer to surrender some Gaza Strip settlements.

Palestinian militants such as Hezbollah persist-ed with their suicide bombings. Their leaders insisted that any peace agreement with Israel would be merely a short-term arrangement. In the end, they insisted, the state of Israel had to be dismantled. Given such intran-sigence on both sides, peace remained as elusive as ever.

11 September 2001: Muslim Al Qaeda terrorists destroy New York's Twin Towers. Claiming over 3,000 vic-tims, the attack gained the terror-ists world-wide recognition but swung US public opinion strongly behind Israel in its own fight against terrorism.

FUTURE UNCERTAIN

CONSEQUENCES OF CONFLICT—
A SUMMARY

The Arab-Israeli conflict has had a profound effect on countless millions of lives in the second half of the twentieth and early twenty-first centuries. The most obvious and unpleasant consequence of the political turmoil is a ceaseless catalogue of human misery. This includes the thousands of soldiers on both sides killed and maimed in war, and the equally large number of civilian casualties who were victims of war, terrorism and reprisals. To this list may be added the shattered lives of refugees, both Palestinian and Lebanese.

The material devastation caused by the conflict has been enormous. Each war saw hundreds of burned out tanks and trucks, aircraft destroyed and houses shattered. Terrorist attacks smashed vehicles and buildings as well as lives, and Israeli counter-measures saw whole blocks of buildings flattened by military bulldozers. The bombs and artillery fire of civil war left Beirut looking like a ghost city.

Coupled with the material destruction is the waste of financial resources channelled into the war effort. In the 1970s, for example, Israel was spending almost a quarter of its wealth on the military at a time when funds were urgently needed for housing, industry, agriculture, education and welfare. In Egypt, Syria, Iraq and Jordan the situation was similar.

Truth and tolerance have been further victims of the conflict. All governments involved fostered a blinkered nationalism, reinforced by censorship, that stifled their citizens' cultural and intellectual lives. Equally worrying was the way the conflict gave rise to intolerant fanaticism, notably militant Zionism in Israel and Muslim extremism. Neither did much to enrich the sum total of human understanding.

The conflict has had broader economic and political consequences. Among these were the divisions

Fuel crisis, 1974. Oil shortages put pressure on the West to reduce its support for Israel and had a devastating effect on the world economy.

in the Arab world that led to such events as the Lebanese and Jordanian civil wars. Nations further afield suffered too. The Cold War intensified as the United States and Soviet Union were drawn onto opposite sides in the struggle. This forced both to increase spending on armaments and military aid. This ultimately helped to bring about the end of communism in Eastern Europe. Two British Prime Ministers – Anthony Eden and Edward Heath – had their ministries cut short as a result of the Arab-Israeli conflict. On a broader scale, the 1956 war hastened the collapse of the vast British and French overseas empires.

The world-wide terrorist campaigns that began in the 1970s, and the economic crisis that followed the 1973 oil embargo and price rise caused a wave of serious economic distress that was felt right around the globe. The United Nations, established in 1945 to guard world peace, was time and again shown by events in the Middle East to be little more than a sounding board for conflicting political agendas. Looking back from the first decade of the twenty-first century, it seems almost incredible that the ill-judged and hasty decisions of 1945-8 could have had such profound and wretched consequences.

LESSONS AND LEGACIES

The tragedy of the Arab-Israeli conflict – or the 'Palestinian Question' as it has become known – is that the longer it continues, the more difficult it becomes to resolve. Each year the toll of injury, hatred, prejudice and fear between the two sides grows higher. Generations have been raised who know nothing but loathing for the other side. More recently, religious fanaticism has brought a new and distinctive bigotry to the conflict.

Yet the struggle has also taught that even in the most unpromising situations reconciliation is possible, although sometimes at a high price. The assassinations of two of the Middle East's great peacemakers, Anwar Sadat and Yitzhak Rabin bore testimony to that. Both died because they realized that, in the long run, their people would be better served by peace than war. The great majority of people on both sides knew this too.

When a settlement is finally reached and historians look back on one of the most bitter conflicts of the modern era, what will they learn? First, that contrary to the prevailing belief at the end of the Second World War, religion remains a vital force that politicians ignore at their peril. Second, that nationalism is as destructive a sentiment as it is a constructive one. Any division of the Earth's surface into self-contained

Travelling in the same direction: US Secretary of State Colin Powell (left) discuses the 'Road Map to Peace' with Israeli Prime Minister Ariel Sharon, 2003.

The West Bank: A Palestinian shepherd tends his flock, surrounded by Israeli villages. Settlements such as these continue to prove an obstacle to reconciliation in a bitterly divided land.

These lessons have to guide any effort ... to reach a comprehensive peace. ... First, the Arab-Israeli conflict is not just a morality between good and evil. It is a complex history, whose resolution requires balancing the needs of both sides ... Second, there is no place for violence, and no military solution to this conflict.'

US President Bill Clinton, 7 January 2001. [Cited in Walter Laquer and Barry Rubin, eds., *The Arab-Israeli Reader*, Penguin, 2001, p. 574.]

units that belong to specific groups of people is artificial, transitory, and contentious. Those who thought that allowing the Jews to have a homeland of their own would solve their problem were proved dreadfully wrong when their fateful decision immediately gave rise to a plethora of further complications.

A third lesson of the conflict will surely be that rapid action on the part of intermediaries is essential when dangerous tensions arise. Had outside forces – the superpowers or the United Nations, for example – been capable of stepping in the moment fighting began in 1948, decades of turmoil might have been avoided. Certainly it would have been easier to find a solution then than later.

Fourthly, and finally, there is the lesson taught by the Israelis in 1948 and the Palestinians during the Intifada. In the end, as in all great movements of history, it is not guns and soldiers that prevail but the collective will of the great majority of the people. Despite all their riot police and rubber bullets, their tanks and rocket-firing gunships, the Israelis could not quell the Palestinian Intifada because a desperate people believed they had nothing to lose. Only when that was recognized was peace possible.

In the end, though, there will remain a powerful and enduring legacy of deep-seated mistrust between the Israelis and the Arabs, especially the Palestinians. On either side, each individual, each family, each community will carry memories and legends of hardship into the future. They will be part of their history, a deep undercurrent liable to emerge and reassert itself in difficult times. In the end, perhaps this legacy will pass into mythology. Until that time, it will remain the most enduring and pernicious consequence of the painful conflict between Arabs and Israelis.

GLOSSARY

Accord
Agreement.

Al-Qaeda
An international Muslim terrorist group, dedicated to opposing by force all non-Muslim governments. Founded by Osama bin Laden in the late 1980s.

Anti-Semitism
Behaviour and beliefs hostile to Jews.

Arab League
Loose co-operation of Arab states formed in 1945.

Authoritarian
Demanding obedience to authority, as in a dictatorship.

Buffer
Land or forces standing between two hostile groups.

Capitalist
Believing in free competition and private enterprise.

Coalition
Group working together.

Coexist
Living together in peace.

Cold War
Period of dangerous tension between the communist East, led by the Soviet Union, and the West led by the US, between 1946 and 1990.

Colony
Overseas territory held by another country.

Communism
Political and economic system based on an all-powerful state and the abolition of private property.

Compromise
Find a middle way between opposing views.

Coup
Forcible overthrow of a government.

Crusades
Attempt by the Christians of Western Europe to capture the Holy Land from the Muslim Turks.

Diaspora
Dispersal of the Jewish people during the Roman era.

Diplomacy
Official negotiation between nations.

Disengage
Draw back from fighting.

Embargo
Ban on trade or a single product.

European Union (EU)
An economic and political alliance between fifteen leading European countries.

Enclave
Isolated piece of territory.

Exterminate
Wipe out.

Faction
Small group within a larger one.

Fanaticism
Excessive devotion to a cause.

Fedayeen
Anti-Israeli Islamic terrorist group established in the 1950s.

Fundamentalist
Person who believes in strict observance of their religion and literal interpretation of religious texts.

Gaza Strip
Narrow strip of land along the eastern shore of the Mediterranean around Gaza City.

General Assembly
Assembly of the United Nations in which all member states have a voice.

Golan Heights
Hills dividing Syria from Israel.

Haganah
Jewish defence force established in Palestine in the 1920s.

Hard-line
Unwilling to compromise.

Hezbollah
Anti-Israeli Islamic terrorist group established in the 1980s.

Hijack
Take over a plane, ship or vehicle by force.

Holocaust
Nazi attempt to wipe out all Jews living in their regime.

Holy Land
Palestine, or, more specifically, the territory around Jerusalem and Bethlehem.

Holy Places
Jerusalem and the places in Palestine mentioned in the Koran and the Bible.

Hostage
Person seized and held illegally against their wishes.

Immigrant
Person who moves into a country to live there.

Imperial
Belonging to an empire.

Infidel
Unbeliever.

Intifada
Palestinian uprising against the Israelis, 1987 and 2000.

Labour
Left-wing Israeli political party.

League of Nations
International organization set up in 1919 to help bring about world peace, understanding and co-operation.

Maim
Permanently injure.

Mandate
Territory governed by another on behalf of the international community.

Mediate
Arrange talks between opponents.

Militant
Aggressive, particularly active in a cause.

Nation state
An independent state, inhabited by people of one nationality.

Partition
Divide up.

PLO
The Palestine Liberation Organization, the principal mouthpiece of the Palestinian people since 1964.

Pre-emptive strike
Attack first when war is certain.

Propaganda
Information slanted to put over one point of view.

Recession
Economic downturn.

Reconciliation
Setting aside differences and making up.

Refugee
A person who flees their homeland.

Revenue
National income.

Rhetoric
High-sounding talk intended to persuade an audience.

Right-wing
Favouring capitalism and free enterprise.

Royal Commission
Official British enquiry.

Scapegoat
Person or a group unfairly held responsible for an action.

Sect
Small and exclusive religious group.

Secular
Non-religious.

Security Council
Decision-making body of the United Nations.

Sinai
Large arid region to the north-east of the Suez Canal.

Soviet Union
Communist state, based around Russia, 1917-1990.

Superpower
Major world power, especially the US and Soviet Union 1945-1990, and thereafter just the US.

Terrorism
The systematic use of violence to achieve a goal.

Third Reich
Nazi regime.

Truce
Temporary cease-fire, usually for negotiations.

Unanimous
With the agreement of everyone concerned.

UNEF
United Nations Emergency Force, sent to the Suez region after the Second Arab-Israeli War.

United Nations
International organization set up in 1945 to help bring about world peace, understanding and co-operation.

War on Terror
The United States campaign to crack down on international terrorism, following the 11 September 2001 attack on New York.

West Bank
Territory lying to the west of the River Jordan.

Zion
The ancient Jewish name for Jerusalem.

Zionism
Militant movement to create an exclusively Jewish homeland in the former mandate of Palestine.

TIMELINE

1891 — First record of trouble between Jews and Arabs in Palestine.

1897 — World Zionist Organisation formed.

1909 — Jewish town of Tel Aviv founded in Palestine.

1914-18 — First World War.

1915 — With British support, Arabs begin revolt against Turks.

1916 — Sykes-Picot Agreement to divide Middle East between Britain and France.

1917 — Balfour declares British support for a Jewish homeland in Palestine.
— British occupy Palestine.

1920-48 — British rule Palestine as a League of Nations mandate.

1920-1 — Arab-Jewish riots in Palestine.

1929 — Arab-Jewish massacres in Palestine.

1933 — Anti-Semitic Nazis to power in Germany.

1936-9 — Major Arab uprising in Palestine.

1937 — Peel Commission recommends partition of Palestine.

1939 — Strict limits on Jewish immigration into Palestine. Second World War (to 1945).

1945 — Arab League formed.

1947 — Britain asks United Nations to sort out Palestine question.
— United Nations votes to partition Palestine.

1948 — British leave Palestine.
— State of Israel proclaimed.
— First Arab-Israeli War (to 1949) inaugurates problem of Palestinian refugees.

1949 — Jordan and Egypt take over parts of Palestine not occupied by Israel.

1952 — Nasser comes to power in Egypt.
— Palestinian terrorist organization *Fatah* formed.

1955 — First Soviet military aid to Arabs.
— NATO sells arms to Israel.
— First Palestinian raids into Israel from Egypt.

1956 — Suez Crisis leads to Second Arab-Israeli War.

1957 — United States proclaims 'Eisenhower Doctrine' of support for non- Communist states in Middle East.

1958 — Egypt and Syria join in United Arab republic (to 1961).

1964 — Palestine Liberation Organization formed.

1967 — Third Arab-Israeli War. Israel occupies West Bank and Gaza Strip, creating many more Palestinian refugees.
— United Nations Resolution 242 calls for Israel to withdraw from occupied territory.

1969 — Yasser Arafat becomes chairman of the PLO.

1969-70 — Israeli-Egyptian War of Attrition.

1970 — Anwar Sadat becomes leader of Egypt.
— Palestinians begin campaign of international terrorism.

— Civil war in Jordan leads to the expulsion of the PLO.

1973 — Fourth Arab-Israeli War.
— Oil-producing Arab states use the 'oil weapon'.

1974 — PLO given responsibility as representative of all Palestinians and recognised as an 'observer' at the United Nations.

1975 — Civil war in Lebanon (to 1990).

1976 — Syrian troops enter Lebanon.

1977 — President Sadat visits Jerusalem.

1978 — United States brokers Camp David Agreement between Egypt and Israel.
— Israeli troops enter Lebanon.

1980-8 — Iran-Iraq War.

1981 — Assassination of President Sadat.

1982 — Israel invades Lebanon (to 1985).
— PLO driven from Lebanon.
— Multinational peacekeeping force into Lebanon.
— Massacre of Palestinians in Lebanese refugee camps.

1987 — First *Intifada* begins.
— Palestinian terrorist group *Hamas* formed.

1988 — Yasser Arafat recognises Israel and renounces violence.

1991 — Gulf War to liberate Kuwait from Iraqi occupation.
— Middle East peace talks begin in Madrid.

1992 — Yitzhak Rabin becomes Prime Minister of Israel.

1993 — PLO and Israel agree Declaration of Principles in Oslo.

1994 — Formal agreements between PLO and Israel to work for peace.
— Palestinian terrorism mounts.
— Israeli troops leave Gaza and some of West Bank.
— Formal peace between Jordan and Israel.

1995 — Zionist extremist assassinates Prime Minister Rabin.

1996 — Arafat elected President of new Palestinian National Authority.
— Israeli Prime Minister Benjamin Netanyahu rejects further concessions to Palestinians as terrorist attacks by Hamas and Islamic Jihad continue.

1999 — Israeli Prime Minister Ehud Barak (Labour) promises to end conflict with Palestinians.

2000 — Formal peace between Israel and Lebanon.
— Second *Intifada* begins.

2001 — Ariel Sharon becomes Israeli Prime Minister.
— Violence mounts on both sides.
— 11 September terrorist attack on New York.
— US President Bush declares war on terrorism.

2002 — Israeli forces reoccupy some of West Bank as bombings and reprisals continue.
— UN, US, Russia and EU put forward a 'roadmap' for peace.

2003 — US-led coalition invades Iraq.

2004 — Progress on 'roadmap' settlement halts as Israel extends security fence and is reluctant to dismantle settlements on the West Bank. Arab suicide bombings continue inside Israel and Israeli-occupied territory.

FURTHER INFORMATION

BOOKS

Suitable for younger readers:

Josh Brooman, *Conflict in Palestine*, Longman, 1990.

Martin Gilbert, *The Arab-Israeli Conflict: Its History in Maps*, Weidenfeld & Nicholson, 1992

Paul Harper, *The Arab-Israeli Conflict*, Wayland, 1989

S. Houston, *The Arab-Israeli Conflict*, Longman, 1989.

John King, *Conflict in the Middle East*, Wayland, 1993

John King, *The Gulf War*, Wayland, 1991

Tony McAleavy, *The Arab-Israeli Conflict*, Cambridge, 1998.

Walter Oppenheim, *The Middle East*, Blackwell, 1989

Stewart Ross, *Witness to History: The Arab-Israeli Conflict*, Heinemann, 2004.

Kirsten E. Schulze, *The Arab-Israeli Conflict*, Pearson, 1999.

For older readers:

Dan Cohn-Sherbok & Dawoud El-Alami, *The Palestine-Israeli Conflict, a Beginner's Guide*, One World, 2001.

Robert Fisk, *Pity the Nation: Lebanon at War*, Andre Deutsch, 1990

Walter Laquer and Barry Rubin, *The Israel-Arab Reader*, Penguin, revised edition, 2001.

Stewart Ross, *Teach Yourself: The Middle East Since 1945*, Hodder Arnold, 2004.

Raja Shehadeh, *When the Bulbul Stopped Singing,* Profile, 2003.

Baylis Thomas, *How Israel Was Won*, Lexington Books, 1999.

Bernard Wasserstein, *Israel & Palestine: Why They Fight and Can They Stop?* Profile, 2003.

WEBSITES

Among the hundreds available, these are among the more reliable:

http://news.bbc.co.uk

http://www.cbc.ca/news

http://edition.cnn.com

http://www.mtholyoke.edu/acad/intrel/me.htm

And giving very different perspectives:

http://electronicintifada.net

http://www.angelfire.com/mi4/angelforisrael

INDEX